BETTING ON SERENITY

How To Win When Your Partner Is Lost To Gambling

HONEY BEAR

The Power Writers Publishing Group

Contents

Preface	vii

Part I
A guide to life with a problem gambler

1. The roller coaster ride that's out of control	3
2. The gambling story never changes	7

Part II
A guide to understanding the problem gambler

3. The gambler: Anatomy and physiology	17
4. The nature of lies	35

Part III
Care of the Concerned Significant Other

5. Killling Your Puppy	45
6. Overwhelm And Victimhood	59
7. Forgiveness	69
8. Shooting Ducks	85
9. Money / Fun With Finance	107
10. Finding Serenity	123
Acknowledgements	133
References	135
Suggested Resources List	137

Published by The Power Writers Publishing Group in 2023.

Honey Bear ©2023.

All Rights Reserved. No part of this book may be reproduced by any mechanical, photographic, or electronic processes, or in the form of a phonographic recording. Nor may be stored in a retrieval system, transmitted or otherwise be copied for public or private use other than for 'fair use' - as brief quotations embodied in articles and reviews, without prior written permission of the publisher.

 A catalogue record for this book is available from the National Library of Australia

ISBN 978-0-6451326-5-6

DISCLAIMER

Any opinions expressed in this work are exclusively those of the author and are not necessarily the views held or endorsed by others quoted throughout. All the information, exercises and concepts contained within this publication are intended for general information only. The author does not take any responsibility for any choices that any individual or organisation may make with this information in the business, personal, financial, familial, or other areas of life based on the choice to use this information. If any individual or organisation does wish to implement the steps discussed herein it is recommended that they obtain their own independent advice specific to their circumstances.

This book is available in print and ebook formats.

BETTING ON SERENITY
How To Win When Your Partner Is Lost To Gambling
HONEY BEAR

"...compulsive gambling...spreads out and affects every person with whom the compulsive gambler is closely involved – his wife, his children, his siblings and parents, his other relatives, his friends and business associates...It is the nature of emotional disorders that when one member of the family is afflicted, the effects are felt by all the others. There are few, however, in which the impact is felt with such severity as in the case of compulsive gambling."

—*Custer and Milt*

Preface

Dear Respected Reader,

Welcome to "Betting on Serenity". This book is based on true events, but is an aggregate of the experiences of a number of different people who, just like you, have found themselves entwined with a compulsive gambler. Our intention is to offer you, the concerned partner, family member or friend of a problem gambler, our own observations and thoughts, as well as a consolidation of the different helpful and guiding teachings that have come our way as we poked and prodded our path through this minefield. What I share with you here are the resources used to rebuild our lives after having been the partner of a compulsive gambler. I hope to help you find a way through the distress and confusion by decreasing your feelings of anxiety and uncertainty. I want you to be able to take back the power that the inner you knows you have, but that you've probably lost touch with because of what is going on around you. The core aim of this book is to help you gain more control of your future.

To be clear and upfront, I am not a counsellor or psychologist. I have no qualifications in either of these fields. However, I do know exactly what it's like to find out that you're living with a compulsive gambler. I've personally done the hard yards of watching my marriage disintegrate and of losing my home. I've dealt with the consequences of another's addiction, and I've done my best to try and 'herd all the cats' and to cover things up so that no-one would find out. Back in the day it was terribly important to me to ensure that everything appeared 'normal' to those on the outside. The distress, the humiliation, the confusion – I've been there and I absolutely understand what you're going through now.

When I was still married to a gambler and searching for help and advice, I felt that while there seemed to be plenty of assistance for the gambler, there seemed to be a real lack of support out there for the gambler's family. I just couldn't find the help that I was after, but meanwhile there seemed to be plenty of help on offer for those admitting to a gambling problem. So, if like me you are looking for some guidance to find your way through the maze, hopefully this book will be like a guiding string that you can follow to help you make your way out.

I vividly remember my ex-husband once telling me that since I was the one who was worried about his gambling, I was the one with the problem. For a long, long time I felt that this was an awfully unfair thing for him to say to me. But with the wisdom of hindsight I can see that he was absolutely right.

When you can fully understand the situation that you find yourself in, and can take responsibility for your part in it, you can start to take back your power, move forward and find peace.

In this book that you are holding now, I am going to walk you through our various journeys. This is how we found our way out of the confusion and frustration that was part and parcel of everyday life while having a partner with a gambling problem. The help and the resources that I in particular was looking for weren't available for me at the time, and so I went out on a hunt to try and find them for myself. This book is the result. It's a guide through the various stages that you may already be in, or will be passing through at some point (for example, forgiveness, looking at your mindset, taking action to move yourself forward and looking at your finances) as well as a bit of more uncomfortable information that you may not want to be thinking about too closely. If I'm honest with myself and with you, I really pushed the whole "gambling package" away into some dark corner of my being, and I guess, then pretended to myself that if I didn't look at it, it would just go away. I thought that if my partner loved me, he would just stop gambling. I thought that if he could see the damage and pain his actions were causing, he would stop gambling. I think that by not facing the need to look into what was driving his gambling, so that I might understand it, I could tell myself that it was a straight forward self-control problem that could be cured with good intention and willpower alone. It's not that easy. It's not that simple. If you truly want your own situation to improve, there are some realities that you will have to stop ignoring. You need to make the commitment to yourself that you will make the effort to face them head on. And that's uncomfortable. To paraphrase the old saying, you'll have to sort out who owns what in the circus, and whose monkeys are whose.

No one else is responsible for your own happiness, and it's absolutely unfair to expect anyone else to take this on for you. If your life plan is going down the toilet, then the person who can turn this around for you is the person who is right here, holding this book and reading these lines in this moment, right now.

Our journey is offered to you in the sincere hope that it will make your own a little easier to manage and navigate. Most of what you'll find here is not about - or indeed for- the gambler; it's about you and what you need to do for yourself. After all, you can't pay someone else to go on a diet for you, or to get up early and go to the gym for you. Some things are your own responsibility, and the person you owe the love, the kindness, the compassion and the consideration to is yourself.

From a place of no judgement I wish you love and light on your journey to the other side of the difficulty you are facing right now. The idea of no judgement and no blame is a core theme of this book. You'll find the words - *No judgement. No condemnation. Just acceptance* - positioned strategically throughout this book. This is my way of reminding you to check in on yourself as you read through the material that follows. Some of it may be hard for you to read, and some of it calls on you to honestly delve into your own circumstances and recognise your feelings. I honour you for stepping up and being fully present to whatever comes up for you as you read on. My heartfelt thanks goes out to those courageous and resilient souls whose very personal stories have contributed to this book. On that note, I want to finish this Preface by sharing the "Serenity Prayer" with you. It has been an incredible support for me. Not to mention being the inspiration for the title of this book.

<u>The Serenity Prayer</u>

*God, grant me the serenity to
Accept the things I cannot Change,
Courage to change the things I can,
And wisdom to know the difference.*

—Reinhold Niebuhr

PART I
A guide to life with a problem gambler

"It is perfectly true, as philosophers say, that life must be understood backwards. But they forget the other proposition, that it must be lived forwards."

—Soren Kirkegaard

ONE

The roller coaster ride that's out of control

I STILL REMEMBER this particular Monday during this particular winter as if it was only yesterday. I was nine months pregnant with baby number two who was due the following week. I remember thinking to myself that if I'd been brave enough, *this* would have been the day that I decided I'd reached my limit: that it was finally time to leave my relationship with a compulsive gambler. The straw that broke the camel's back was finding out that our joint account was not only completely empty, but that it had been overdrawn and was hundreds of dollars in the red. The thing is though that I didn't leave. I had a toddler. I had a new baby on the way, due in eight days time. My family were coming to stay for the happy event, and a scheduled caesarean meant that I wouldn't be able to drive for a few weeks afterwards. So, how did I feel? Trapped, let down (yet again), angry, exasperated, powerless, lost and overwhelmed. How was I going to extricate myself from this mess that I'd allowed myself to get into, and yet that I felt someone else was largely responsible for? So many questions were whirling around in my head. Unfortunately, not many answers were coming back.

As well as being angry at my gambling husband, I was also angry at myself, because sadly this was not my first rodeo. We'd been together for a good number of years, before I first twigged to the fact that he had a gambling problem. By the time baby number two was due, I was well and truly aware of the elephant in the room. So I really had no-one else to blame for the situation I was in – not that I thought of it that way at the time though. But then they do say that hindsight is 20:20.

As it turned out, things got worse after this, before they got any better. But get better they most certainly did, and the disaster that my life had become ultimately propelled me forward to a life that I couldn't possibly have had (or even imagined) if things had just chugged along in the same old way and I had spent the rest of my life maintaining the status quo. The 'disaster' turned out to be an absolute blessing which has been giving back to me in spades ever since I took my own power back.

As I said, this was not the first time that being married to a compulsive gambler had left me feeling trapped, swamped, angry, frustrated, etc, etc, etc. (add in your own favourite depressing adjective). When I finally reached out to outside sources for help and support I found that while there was plenty of it out there for the gamblers themselves, there wasn't a whole lot out there for the long suffering partner. The often repeated response usually went along the lines of "we used to have a service, but it's no longer running" and "We used to have a support group, but it has folded." So what did I do to help myself? When things finally went completely pear-shaped (he walked out, leaving me literally holding the baby), I turned to books and DVDs and anything else that I could find that I thought was relevant and could help me. Exactly what I was after, I didn't really find, but I love getting lost in a good book, and so I cast my net wide and read and listened to whatever I felt sounded like it may offer what I was looking for.

Having struggled to find the type of help that *I* was after, my aim here is to gently bring you along on a walk through what myself and others have found practical and helpful, and outline for you how I went from dumped ex of a gambling addict and wondering how I was going to feed two kids on $3.10, to being someone who now feels financially stable and is keeping on an upward trajectory. I absolutely believe I have a very good life now as well as my future ahead being one to look forward to, rather than dreading. So if you're on the downhill slope on life's great big roller coaster and you don't know if it's going to hold onto the rails or fling you off into oblivion, or even if you're only a little uncomfortable with the status quo (and that's fine too) and are just curious, then hopefully what we've learned along the way will help you too.

No Judgement. No condemnation. Just acceptance.

As the late great Jim Rohn said in one of his stories, if you're on a road late at night and someone is waving a lamp in the middle of a storm to warn you that the bridge ahead has collapsed and you need to turn around and go back the other way, are you going to say "You don't have a clue what you're talking about! I'll be fine!" Or might you say "Thanks so much for the heads-up! I think I'll turn back around and keep my feet dry!" So whether you're someone who's casting a cautious eye to the future, or someone who's running like hell from the past, the pages that follow offer you what we've discovered during and after life with a partner dedicated to the relentless pursuit of losing.

"Gambling is the son of avarice and the father of despair."

–French Proverb

TWO

The gambling story never changes

I HAVE a vivid memory of going to visit a gambling counsellor, long after my husband had left us. I happened to see a short article in the paper about a local gambling counselling service that had received some funding from the government and so was able to offer consultations. With young children to bring up I was very highly motivated to track down expert advice on how best to steer them away from following in their father's footsteps. It may have been a bit selfish of me, but I thought that if there was money out there to help gamblers with their problem, then I thought it was entirely fair for me to turn up for my slice of that particular pie. I was a "victim" of gambling after all. The counsellor drew a diagram for me on a large whiteboard and explained the cycle of gambling behaviour. He then used the same diagram to describe how I had been acting at the various points in the cycle in response to my partner's gambling. I wish I'd copied it down at the time, because it seemed to nail my situation almost completely. Rather scarily, he was *very* accurate! I can still remember saying to him "It's like you had a hidden microphone in our house!" He just slowly shook his head and said with the weary voice of someone who'd heard it all a thousand times before: "The story NEVER changes!"

So then, if the story never changes, it's more than likely that you're going through the same experiences, feeling the same emotions, and dealing with the same crappy fallout that I was. I certainly don't claim to have all the answers, but along the way, myself and others in the same boat have found some. As I worked my way forward, I found myself continually presented with guidance in the form of anything from books to life experiences to little synchronicities. Serendipity was often working very hard on my behalf, and I've learned an awful lot. Some of the knowledge I could have definitely done with many years earlier! But, as a wise person once said, we are the people who we are now as a result of our combined life experiences up to this point. I freely admit that I did manage to ignore some very excellent advice along the way though, through the application of some very twisted logic. It seems that it is as the sales textbooks tell us: we make decisions with emotion and then try to defend them with logic. Great if you're selling. Potentially rather unsettling though if you're left making the repayments after deciding to buy.

"How's the serenity?" is one of my favourite movie quotes. This absolute classic of the Australian comedy genre called '*The Castle*' is about the Kerrigan family. This happy go lucky working-class clan was lucky enough to have a holiday home at a place called Bonnie Doon. The family's patriarch Darryl Kerrigan would often say "How's the serenity" to express his heartfelt feelings of peace and tranquillity on his family visits to Bonnie Doon.

I remember when I was growing up that my grandfather had a framed copy of the *Serenity Prayer* by Reinhold Neibuhr on his wall. I suppose that having seen it so often it just became part of the background, and while I thought it was nice enough, I never understood why people thought it was so wonderful and profound. About a year and a bit after my partner had left, I was sitting on the loungeroom floor of my new home, going through some boxes that I'd packed my life into while I was renting a little flat after losing the family home. I came across some handouts that I'd been given by a financial counsellor who I'd seen many years before, and one of these was the *Serenity Prayer*. Interestingly enough I later discovered that this prayer had actually been adopted by Alcoholics Anonymous. I still remember feeling the jolt of a real "a-ha" moment when things finally clicked into place and I *finally* understood the serenity prayer: the serenity to *accept* the things I could not change, the *courage* to change the things I could, and the wisdom to *know the difference*. Honestly, if there's only one thing you get out of reading this book, let it be an understanding that getting to a place where you can accept that there are things which really *are* beyond your ability to change, will take a whole lot of pressure off you. If you can accept this, let it go and move on, then you're on your way to your own Bonnie Doon. That's serenity. That's peace with yourself and your life.

No Judgement. No condemnation. Just acceptance.

Having walked a few miles in your shoes, I know where they pinch. I know that your partner's gambling has you all churned up, otherwise it may not be likely that you'd be reading this book. The gambler I used to live with had a habit of saying "If you throw enough money at a problem you can make it go away." Despite his certainty about this, I don't think he was quite right. I believe that there are definitely some things that even with the best will in the world, no amount of money is *ever* going to fix. No matter how much lipstick and taffeta you put on it, a pig in a prom dress will always be just a smelly farm animal wearing a shiny dress. Mind you, I'd also guess that it's more comfortable to be sad and miserable living in a mansion than being sad and miserable sheltering in a cardboard box under a bridge at the dodgy end of town, especially when it's pouring down with rain.

Feeling Like An Egg In A Bottle

For a number of reasons, for a very long time I felt trapped in my life with a gambler. A bit like the boiled egg sucked into Professor

Julius Sumner-Miller's milk bottle by the burning flame. If you don't know who this brilliant teacher was, Google is your friend - check him out. The only difference I think was that my milk bottle was frosted glass, so I couldn't see my way out, and the label with the escape instructions was stuck on the outside, so I couldn't read that either. So how does the egg become set free from its glass prison? Well, if you want to get it back out in one piece, if you can put enough pressure behind it, it will pop out whole. If the fast high pressure approach doesn't work, the other way is to mash it up and get it out in little bits. But smashed up egg isn't that appetising is it? So how do we make it more appealing? I used to work not too far from a café that made the most excellent egg and mayo bap on the planet, and I was probably one of their best customers. "Lucy's Special Egg" was a delicious mix of mashed egg with added mayo, chopped celery, spring onion, salt and pepper and a little bit of some secret magic which made the whole creation taste just sensational. Even if you don't come out of your relationship with a compulsive gambler as an unscathed whole, you too can go from "trapped" to "smashed" to "smashing", where your end result can be so much better than your starting point.

No Judgement. No condemnation. Just acceptance.

So What Is Your Starting Point?

If you think of your situation with your problem gambler as being a bit like you being stuck in a mouse trap, it helps to know what kind of mouse trap you are in, so that you can think about getting out. Consider the following three different kinds of mouse trap on the market, and see if you can gain insight into the situation you are in (beyond "living the dream") on a day to day basis.

- The first kind of mouse trap is the traditional snappy trap. You know the one - mouse nibbles cheese, trap is tripped and wire bar snaps back to kill the mouse. This kind of trap

I equate with the person who, when they find out that they are tied up with a compulsive gambler, decides to cut their losses early on. Their personal values and future plans get snapped in half and so they decide to salvage what they can and leave post-haste.

- Trap number two is the really nasty sticky type of trap. From a welfare point of view these ones are just horrendous. With this type of trap your unsuspecting mouse walks onto a super sticky surface and gets stuck there. They can't move their little feet, and so are forced to stay there and starve to death. Or they may get dispatched in some way or other if they are found. This is how I used to feel – stuck and I couldn't get out. Well, not without causing more grief than was already in the mix (or so I thought). If you're still living with a gambler and feel stuck and can't move, this may be the type of trap you are in.

- Mouse trap number three is the humane type of trap where the mouse simply walks into a small dark box and gets trapped inside. He stays there until someone comes along and takes him outside and releases him into the shrubbery. Looking back now, I think the reality is that I spent a lot of time in trap number 2 then graduated to trap number 3. By leaving us, my husband released me from the confines of the sticky trap and enabled me to go exploring the wider world on my own and find much better things that were out there. If you are also one of the lucky ones whose partner leaves voluntarily, this could represent the scenario you are in.

So then, if you're ready, would you like to fix yourself a nice cup of tea and a biscuit, settle down, and let's look into how you can go from crappy to happy? Let's get you going from feeling you're stuffed to knowing your stuff, and then move forward with it.

Wouldn't you rather be able to regularly indulge in some loose leaf Royal Blend from Fortnum and Mason than to be having to make do with anonymous unbranded cheap and nasty tea bags made from the leftover sweepings from the factory floor? I know which option I'd be choosing! Fair warning though, as we move through these chapters you'll probably have to face up to some truths about yourself that you don't want to see. "If I can't see it, I can pretend it's not real and that gives me an excuse not to do anything about it." How much do you stand to lose if you don't ask yourself some hard questions? Is doing nothing a risk that you are willing to take? Can you ask yourself, "what do I believe to be true that maybe isn't?"

Ready? Buckle up then and let's go! Put pen to paper and answer the following:

Guestimate the number of years that you think you have left on this mortal coil.

How many of these are you prepared to continue spending living in worry and distress?

How many do you want to spend not living that way?

List 10 (or more!) things that frustrate you about living with a compulsive gambler.

1...

2...

3...

4...

5...

6...

7...

8..

9..

10..

Are you prepared to take some action to gain some relief from the list of frustrations you've just admitted to above?

PART II
A guide to understanding the problem gambler

*"A gambler never makes the same mistake twice.
It's usually three or more times."*

—Terrence Murphy

THREE

The gambler: Anatomy and physiology

OKAY THEN, before we pin our gambler to the corkboard and start dissecting him/her to find out what makes them tick, let's open our anatomy manual at the beginning and start with some basic definitions. That way we can all be on the same page when we start peeling back the layers of our well pickled specimen.

What Is Gambling?

The Cambridge dictionary tells us that to gamble is to do something that involves risk that might result in loss of money or failure, hoping to get money or achieve success. It is thought to be derived from the early 18th century word 'gamel', meaning to play games. So then, it looks like we can essentially break gambling down into a few basic elements: wagering something of value (usually money) on the chance (uncertain outcome) of winning a prize or gain of some kind (again, usually money).

To our gambling friends the bird in the hand is nowhere near worth the two they can see in the bush. They have probably already developed their own 'system' whereby they believe that they can trade the one bird that they definitely do have, and not only manage to catch the other two (who are odds-on more wily than the gambler and won't be caught for quids), but also somehow manage to get back the bird they originally had. This bird however usually shoots through the first chance it gets and is never seen again! It's like the speeding arrow or the spoken word – it can't be called back. From what I've seen, this is about the only certainty with the whole gambling shenanigans. Nowhere have I yet found a definition which equates "gambling" with "winning".

No Judgement. No condemnation. Just acceptance.

Now that we've got our starting point for what gambling is, let's bravely go exploring down the dark path a little further...

There are many different ways to risk your money gambling, and broadly speaking these have the potential to give either an *instant* reward or a *delayed* reward. The instant types of rewards would be the scratchies, the pokies, or betting on horse racing. You hand over your money and you get your result pretty quickly. Bingo! Instant gratification! Types of gambling which entail a delayed potential reward are things like playing Lotto or buying art union tickets. In these examples, you buy your ticket, but then need to wait a while (sometimes days to weeks) for the result. There's a decent time separation between your wager and the event you've risked your money on. People are more likely to lose obscene amounts of money on the former, rather than the latter.

Moving back to probing a little deeper into our gambling specimen, according to work by Dr Samantha Thomas for the Office of Gaming and Racing, Victorian Department of Justice, it appears that there are three basic types of gambler and they interact with gambling in different ways. First, you have your low-risk gambler. This is the person who is afraid of losing money and so doesn't engage in gambling to a significant degree. Next, we have our moderate-risk gamblers. These ones want to win, but they tend to see gambling more as a social activity. These ones are typically young men who engage in sports betting. I tend to think of them as the guys who move in flocks (i.e. the sheep) at events such as the rugby for example, where Pretty Young Things in short shorts (i.e. the foxes) move through the crowd tempting them with the handy little mobile betting devices that come right to them, rather than them having to make the effort to walk up to a betting counter to place a wager. Not only is this more convenient and likely to inspire impulse betting, but the young women that I've seen employed in these roles are significantly more alluring than "Old Dave" who works behind the counter. What's not to like, especially if you've had a few refreshing beverages beforehand and are feeling a bit merry, not to mention being keen to look like the big man in front of your mates? And these days, you can do all this on your phone. Too easy!

Thirdly, we have the problem gamblers. These are the ones who instead of just *wanting* to win, they *need* to win to recover their losses. Many of the moderate-risk gamblers can move in and out of the problem gambling group if they binge. Apparently they believe that they should be able to control themselves and their gambling. I guess if you're reading this book, you know how well that works out for them (or not)!

Now then, let's move on to our next definition: the 'gambler's fallacy'. According to the APA Dictionary of Psychology this is "a failure to recognise the independence of chance events, leading to the mistaken belief that one can predict the outcome of a chance event on the basis of the outcome of past chance events." For example, if you toss a coin in the air there's a 1 in 2 chance that it will land on 'heads'. Heads or tails are your only two options. So even if it comes up heads six times in a row, the odds of it being 'tails' on the next throw are never going to be higher than 1 in 2, no matter how much someone may want it to be something different.

The Diagnostic and Statistical Manual of Mental Disorders, 5th Edition, (DSM-5) talks about patterns of gambling. Gambling may be a regular thing, or it may be irregular. Gamblers may be persistently honing their craft, or they may be in remission. They can run the gamut from bouts of heavy gambling to times of complete abstinence and apparently even periods of unproblematic gambling.

Allegedly, they can even have spontaneous long-term remissions. Blimey! I think I just about fell off my unicorn when I read that bit! Your faith in your gambler is not all lost however, because when in this mythical period of spontaneous remission, it seems that they can then go back to thinking that they can control their gambling and can gamble on some things with no problem at all – and end up returning to being a problem gambler again. Ahhh, there we go, safe back in 'reality land' with our unicorn tucked safely away in it's nice warm stable!

Moving on from this cynical (or realistic?) point of view then and progressing to the more meaty stuff, the APA College dictionary tells us that 'pathological gambling' is an impulse-control disorder characterised by chronic, maladaptive wagering, leading to significant interpersonal, professional, or financial difficulties. I quite like that term 'maladaptive wagering'. It sounds like a great name for a racehorse! If I was to ever become a racehorse owner, I think that's what my first one would be called. Either that or 'Rank Stupidity'. I'm not sure which. Maybe I'll have to toss a coin to decide. I'm really very sure though, that the "significant interpersonal, professional or financial difficulties" are all sounding horribly familiar to you – they certainly are to me and the other brave souls whose stories are included in this book! These are like three horsemen of the apocalypse. Weren't there four horsemen you ask? Well, the fourth one found that he couldn't go past an open betting shop without feeling that he just had to stop off and place a few bets - so he's completely oblivious to the havoc his three mates are busy wreaking out in the real world.

Is this feeling like the kind of territory you've been trying to navigate your way through? If so, you're in the right place. Shall we walk on together then? We shall!

No Judgement. No condemnation. Just acceptance.

Now that we've reached the Land of the Excessive Gambler, we can break the inhabitants of this dark, depressive territory into two major types: your action gamblers and your escape gamblers. According to *Addiction: A reference Encylopaedia*, action gamblers are addicted to the rush of excitement that they get from gambling. Their preferred method for losing money hand over fist is to bet on things that require a degree of skill and are highly interactive – like Blackjack for example.

The opposite of your action gambler is the escape gambler. For these people their excessive gambling is all about tuning out and forgetting their problems. Escape gamblers tend to like passive forms of gambling, like playing poker machines. I had no idea just *how* passive pokie gambling could be until one evening many years ago, when I saw someone 'playing' a pokie by wedging a torn off piece of a beer coaster down the side of one of the buttons, so that the machine just continually ticked over and over and chewed through his money at what I thought was a frighteningly obscene rate, while he sat there drinking his beer and smoking a cigarette. Without even touching the machine he was able to watch it churning through his money with the help of just a small piece of cardboard.

Field Guide To Problem Gamblers

What Do They Look Like?

Is there an average Joe or Jo problem gambler? According to the Senate Committee Gambling Reform Report, 2012, the risk factors for problem gamblers include being male, and being divorced or separated. Males tend to be more impulsive than females, so they tend to be at a higher risk of developing gambling problems because they take more risks than women do. Age is also a factor, as the earlier someone starts gambling, the higher the likelihood that problems will develop, and just like drugs or alcohol it can start during adolescence while the brain is still maturing. It's common for people who are problem gamblers to have had a large win (i.e. a very positive experience) with gambling quite early on. Having said that, there also appear to be no hard and fast rules that dictate why some people go on to become compulsive gamblers while other don't.

Males are more likely than females to start gambling early on in life, but whichever sex you are, if you have a problem with gambling you're more likely to have gradual increases in the frequency of your gambling and the amount of money you are betting. Generally speaking, it will take years for problem gambling to develop. Women who are gamblers tend to start later in life than men, but they become problem gamblers more quickly than men do. Men are more likely to bet on things like sports, horse racing and cards, whereas women are more likely to play the pokies.

Distorted thought processes seem to be a common finding when we look under the hood of the problem gambler. They can be in denial (you can probably tick that box!), they can have some funny superstitions, and their carefully honed and crafted 'system' can give them a sense that they have some power or control over the outcome of random events which in reality they have no power or control over at all. The ex-partner of one of the contributors here apparently used to be of the opinion that the second favourite horse in a race was more likely to come in first than the favourite was, and when he was gambling on roulette he was seen to be quite faithful to his favourite block of five or six numbers on the wheel.

They can also be overconfident and cocky people. Some gamblers may be impulsive, restless and easily bored (hmmm, sounds familiar to me – how about you?). They may be very concerned about gaining and keeping the approval of others and can be extravagantly generous when they are in a winning patch. Other gamblers though may be depressed and lonely, and might gamble when they are feeling helpless or depressed. It has also been suggested that stressful life events can have a role in triggering problem gambling, but then again, I'm sure we all know plenty of people in our circle who have gone through some very stressful times and haven't gone on to develop a gambling addiction. If you've got a gambler who likes to follow the horses, work by Dickerson has found that frequent gamblers are more likely to place bets at the last minute before the start of a race. This has certainly been my experience. Do you remember how fast the cricketer David Boone could move when he was fielding in the slips? Someone else I know has described her ex as moving just as fast when he had the right motivation. She had vivid memories of him in the betting shop frantically filling in a betting slip at one counter, and then leaping across the room at full tilt to feed the all-important bits of paper into the machine on the opposite counter, hit the button on top of it and plonk the money down, all before the horses burst out of the starting stalls. A nanosecond too slow and all that effort would be in vain.

No Judgement. No condemnation. Just acceptance.

One thing many compulsive gamblers do have in common is the belief that money is the root cause of, and the shining solution to their problems. This certainly seemed to be the conviction that one lady's gambling partner had. If she brought up his gambling, or the resulting climbing debts, he'd get shirty and simply make his standard belligerent reply that he was "sorry that he didn't earn as much money as xyz!" Interestingly enough, it was always some relative of hers that was referred to as 'xyz'. He just never seemed to understand that the money was a secondary issue in the whole big picture. Speaking for myself, it was the lying, the deceit, the betrayal and all the other garbage that went along with the gambling that was my main cause of distress.

> *"The core pathology of problem gambling is a belief that one can win money in the long term."*
>
> —*(Senate Committee – Gambling Reform Report 2012)*

So, How Do I Tell If I'm Living With A Problem Gambler?

Well yes. I have to admit that this probably looks like the world's dumbest question! If you're living with a problem gambler, then I'm reasonably certain that you already have a pretty fair idea of which direction the wind is blowing! Maybe though, it's early on in your relationship and so you may just be having some doubts or uneasy feelings.

The DSM-5 uses the term 'gambling disorder' for pathological gambling, and categorises it as a nonsubstance-related addiction rather than an impulse–control disorder. This definition has come from a growing body of evidence showing that gambling behaviours activate similar reward systems in the brain to those which are activated by drugs of abuse. Along with this, there are some behavioural symptoms which appear to be comparable to those seen with substance abuse disorders, such as alcohol and drug abuse. For example, drugs like cocaine can directly activate the reward system in the brain. This is important because the reward system is involved in reinforcing behaviours and making memories. Drugs typically activate this reward system and produce feelings of pleasure (the "high") so intensely that normal activities can go out the window.

The following description of gambling disorder comes directly from the DSM-5 manual:

"Persistent and recurrent problematic gambling behaviour leading to clinically significant impairment or distress, as indicated by the individual exhibiting four (or more) of the following in a 12-month period:

- Needs to gamble with increasing amounts of money in order to achieve the desired excitement.
- Is restless or irritable when attempting to cut down or stop gambling.
- Has made repeated unsuccessful efforts to control, cut back, or stop gambling.
- Is often preoccupied with gambling (e.g. having persistent thoughts of reliving past gambling experiences, handicapping or planning the next venture, thinking of ways to get money with which to gamble).
- Often gambles when feeling distressed (e.g. helpless, guilty, anxious, depressed).

- After losing money gambling, often returns another day to get even ("chasing" one's losses).
- Lies to conceal the extent of involvement with gambling.
- Has jeopardised or lost a significant relationship, job, or educational or career opportunity because of gambling.
- Relies on others to provide money to relieve desperate financial situations caused by gambling."

The severity of the gambling is considered mild if four or five of the above criteria are met, moderate if six or seven criteria are met, and severe if eight or nine criteria are met. From this list, the ones that are most frequently met are usually related to a preoccupation with gambling and "chasing" losses.

The DSM 5 then goes on to define the gambling as either episodic or persistent. Episodic gambling is described as meeting diagnostic criteria at more than one time point, with symptoms subsiding between periods of gambling disorder for at least several months. The gambling is considered to be persistent if the gambler experiences continuous symptoms and meets the diagnostic criteria for multiple years.

Chasing The Loss

I know this probably looks pretty self-explanatory also, but using greyhound racing as an example, let's think of the "loss" as the rabbit and the gambler as the greyhound chasing after the rabbit.

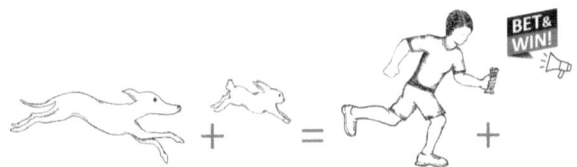

Page one of "Book of the greyhound": the greyhound always *chases* the rabbit. The greyhound never catches the rabbit (at least not at the races held in public).

When the pattern of "chasing one's losses" develops, gamblers have an urgent need to keep on gambling, and will often place larger bets or take greater risks to try and overturn a loss (or lots of losses). They might even ditch their precious gambling strategy and try to win back their losses all at once. Although a lot of gamblers may "chase" their losses for short periods of time, it is the persistent, and often long-term, "chase" that indicates a gambling disorder.

The Gambling Cycle

There are various versions of the 'gambling cycle', but the essentials are in the diagram below. This cycle of problem gambling was developed by Mitchell Brown.

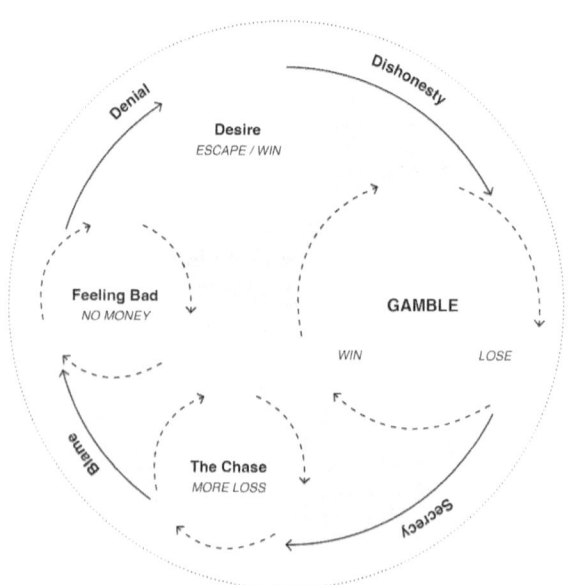

If we start at the top then, gambling can seem to offer an escape from emotional stresses or boredom, because as we've seen it can change people's mood - for a short time at least. Of course they may also be gambling because they want money. If they have a big win when they start gambling, it can lead them on to more gambling, as the win reinforces their belief that gambling is a good way to get money. If they lose however, this can lead to them chasing their losses. Essentially they are trying to fix their problem using the same method that caused the problem in the first place. You know how well that works out, don't you? The accumulated losses then bring the gambler to an emotional crisis where they have great feelings of remorse and sorrow for the problems their gambling has caused themselves and their loved ones. I don't think my partner ever came within a bull's roar of this, but apparently it is part and parcel of the gambling package. Going back to the cycle then, the growing financial crisis caused by the gambling leads to…more gambling.

No Judgement. No condemnation. Just acceptance.

Like ripples on a pond, the actions of the gambler radiate out and affect more people than just themselves. According to Chris Lobsinger and Lynn Bechett who wrote the book "Odds on to break even: a practical approach to gambling awareness", estimates indicate that every pathological gambler will directly affect the lives of eight to ten other people. That's a lot of people don't you think? This list includes spouses and other immediate family members such as their children, parents and siblings, as well as employers and co-workers. More distant relatives may also be influenced by the actions of the problem gambler, and even complete strangers may be negatively affected if there are also illicit activities connected to the gambling.

Gamblers will often lie to family members, therapists, or others to conceal the extent of their involvement with gambling. These instances of deceit may also include covering up illegal behaviours such as forgery, fraud, theft, or embezzlement to obtain money with which to gamble. They may also engage in "bailout" behaviour, turning to family members or others for help with a desperate financial situation that was caused by gambling. Remember – if you have a close relationship with a gambler, it's probably easier for them to get money from you than from someone they don't know very well. The less energy they have to expend, the better.

They can also use guilt to control you. If your experience has been anything like mine, I'm sure you will have had more than one guilt trip laid on you by your gambler. The spiritual author Stuart Wilde says that when we worry about what people think of us, we place control in *their* opinions and *their* reactions, and this disempowers our own values. Once they've used guilt to hook you emotionally, you'll find it hard to break free, and any escape you do manage to pull off will usually involve a big fight. After all, who would want to give up a good cash cow that pays out for you when you play the guilt card, and can probably be induced to pay out a bit better when you add a hissy fit to the guilt trip? Winner, winner chicken dinner!

A Tale Of Two Neurotransmitters

When my former partner was gambling I was completely flummoxed as to *why* he just kept on gambling, when (I thought) Blind Freddy could have seen the hurt and pain it was causing me, and the joint account balance spelled it out rather clearly in black and white. I really believed that if he actually *wanted* to change his gambling behaviour, then it was simply a matter of making the decision to do so and then following through on it.

It was about a year after he left that I first came across the connection between brain chemistry and compulsive behaviours. I was at a conference and heard someone speak about research into the reasons behind drug addicts having relapses. It was a bit like flipping a switch. I suddenly went from thinking compulsive gambling was all down to lack of self-discipline, to beginning to think that it could at least partly be due to brain chemicals going a bit haywire. I began to get this mental image of a cartoon brain floating around on its back in a swimming pool full of hormones, while occasionally lifting itself up to take a sip from some exotic cocktail.

As mentioned earlier, according to the Senate committee Gambling reform report 2012, science is finding growing evidence that there are many similarities between pathological gambling and substance abuse disorder, especially when looking at the brain's reward centre. Treatments such as a 12 step programme seem to be helpful for gamblers as well as alcoholics. I guess that makes sense because there are cravings and highs in response to gambling, just as there are to drugs or alcohol. Lesieur describes gamblers talking about their wins and losses in emotional terms such as "high" or "downer".

Neurotransmitters are little chemical messengers which our body makes for itself. In a normally functioning brain neurotransmitters are released, they then activate a receptor, and then their action is stopped when they break down or move away. If any of these processes is disturbed, that's when you can get problems. While the neurotransmitter story is a complex one, the two that I'll briefly introduce you to here are serotonin and dopamine.

Serotonin is a neurotransmitter linked to impulse control. It can affect our energy levels and mood and can contribute to feelings of well-being. It has a role in how we cope with and learn from adverse events, by inhibiting similar behaviour following a 'punishment'. Researchers including Bullock and Potenza have shown that low levels of serotonin have been found in problem gamblers.

Dopamine is involved in rewarding and reinforcing behaviours. It is responsible for our drive to acquire things such as food, drugs or even achievement. It is associated with pleasure and reward. Prolonged and intense stimulation of the dopamine receptors is part of the addiction process.

People who are addicted may seek out 'rewards' such as gambling. This can then cause the release of dopamine which triggers feelings of pleasure. Bullock and Potenza say that both the probability of a reward and the magnitude of a possible reward are two key components of gambling. Higher sustained levels of dopamine during periods of increased uncertainty of reward and higher variability in the size of the reward may contribute to compulsive gambling (we'll revisit this concept later on but with a slightly different spin on it). Because dopamine has also been linked to impulsivity it may contribute to problem gambling via this mechanism too. When looking at gambling to recover losses, serotonin seems to promote loss chasing as a behavioural option, and dopamine seems to produce complex changes in the perception of the value of the losses which the gambler judges to be worth chasing.

Withdrawal And Tolerance

Let's have a look at withdrawal and tolerance now. Withdrawal is what happens when someone stops taking their drugs, or the gambler stops gambling. They develop feelings which are the opposite of what they felt when they were taking drugs or gambling. According to Wray and Dickerson, the most commonly reported symptoms that Gamblers Anonymous members described when they stopped betting were irritability, restlessness, depressed mood, poor concentration and obsessional thoughts. When an addict stops taking drugs or gambling, the dopamine receptor levels can be suppressed for months and months – they don't bounce back to normal as soon as they stop. This means that the brain of an addict will function differently for a long time. Repeatedly taking drugs or gambling means that the brain will adapt by changing its sensitisation and tolerance levels. Essentially, you need more and more drugs over time to produce the same response, or looking at it another way, the same dose produces less of a response. If you think about it, if it's the act of gambling that gives you the buzz, why not gamble with one dollar, rather than shell out hundreds of them?

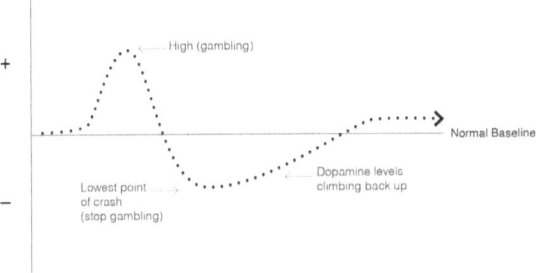

The diagram above is a very simplified attempt to give you a visual picture of the description above. When they start gambling, the dopamine levels go up (the "high"). When they stop, they go down (the "downer), but it takes them a long time just to recover back to a normal level.

So then let's sum up the commonalities between substance addiction and gambling addiction. These were nicely outlined in Jim Orford's book *Excessive Appetites:*

- The activity dominates the person's thinking, feeling and behaviour

- They get a rush or a pleasurable change in mood as a result of engaging in the behaviour

- They seem to need increased amounts of the activity to get the same effect

- They experience withdrawal symptoms if the activity is suddenly reduced or stopped

- There is conflict with those around them

- There can be a relapse of the activity even after a long period of not engaging in it.

Brain chemistry is complicated, but hopefully this may help you to understand a part of the reason why your gambler keeps on gambling. Being on the outside looking in, I found it impossible to understand the whole gambling psyche. It just made absolutely no sense to me whatsoever. Not that it's an excuse, but I think knowing that brain chemistry has a part to play may help put some pieces of the puzzle together for you, and it's something that I had my head in the sand about for a very, very long time.

"A lie told often enough becomes the truth."

—Vladimir Lenin

FOUR

The nature of lies

SO, how do you feel about being lied to? It's not that great is it? Having 'lived the dream' for a number of years, I came to the realisation that gambling and lying go hand in glove like country and western, tea and biscuits and Marks and Spencer.

Lies, Lies And More Lies

As much as the sheer waste of money was distressing to me, I think the accompanying lies, the deceit and the utter bullshit that was spouted wounded the core of my being much, much more. I think a little part of my spirit died each time I heard my husband's lies, and an equal part of my self-respect went with it each time I pretended to believe them for the sake of keeping the peace. I have to admit that my partner was actually a phenomenally perceptive people-reader, and so I think he knew when I'd reached the point where any remnants of hope were gone and my heart just wasn't in it any more each time I feigned belief in whatever the particular lie of the moment was. Is any of this sounding familiar to you? Am I hitting any raw nerves?

No Judgement. No condemnation. Just acceptance.

Make no mistake, compulsive gamblers are compulsive liars. After all, they have to be don't they? Constantly having to feed an addiction is not normal behaviour, so to project an outward appearance of normality, you have to be doing some pretty good jiggery-pokery to make sure that the house of straw somehow looks like it's made of solid brick. I guess it's a matter of expertise in relation to the good old acronym CYA: Cover Your Arse. Which is very good advice when you think of it. Mind you, trying to cover a six foot wide gap with a piece of dental floss doesn't really manage to cut the mustard. That's asking for one hell of a parallax error on the part of the observer! All jokes aside though, the reality is that the more the gambler can keep hidden, the longer they can keep up their gambling without having to face the consequences. As a counsellor once pointed out to me when I was feeling like a bit of a dill about being suckered in in the first place, if these people went around with the words 'con man' tattooed on their forehead, they wouldn't be half as good as they are at what they do. So don't beat yourself up too much if you've been taken in. In the history of the world you weren't the first, and you certainly won't be the last.

The gambler I lived with always very good at coming up with stories, and they always sounded convincing to varying degrees, so it was often hard to catch him out in an obvious lie. I must admit, I did keep hearing various things that he said to me early on in the relationship and thinking to myself "that doesn't quite sound right – but why would he lie to me," or "that just doesn't feel right- but why would he lie to me?" Well, there were two reasons really: 1) because he could, and 2) because he thought I would believe and trust in him. He was right on both counts. Growing up I was either carefully protected from people like him, or they just never crossed my path. So when I did meet someone with a black belt level of skill in deceit, I didn't recognise him for what he was. What's more I had no experience or tools in my 'experience bag' to deal with where I'd found myself, and so I failed spectacularly. I may not be Robinson Crusoe here, because someone else that I know had a partner who used to joke that if she ever wrote her autobiography she should call it "Gullible's Travels." On second thoughts… maybe he wasn't joking…

Fast forward a bit, and when I had to face the bleeding obvious because there was money disappearing out of the joint account in $200 lots, being withdrawn in quick succession from the cashpoint outside the local betting shop, I had to stop and ask him about it. What was he spending the money on, and why did he keep making multiple withdrawals for the same amount within short times of each other? Well, his story was that he was taking the money out to pay "bills". And then he'd forgotten that there was another 'bill' he had to pay, and then there was another one! Gosh! So many bills for him to pay! But what bills were these I would ask myself? We had a joint account to pay the bills – electricity, rates, water, phone and so on. What were these other bills that had seemingly popped up out of nowhere needing to be paid? More to the point, why didn't I ask him these questions? The answer I think is two-fold. First, I hate conflict, and would rather run a mile in ill- fitting stilettos than have to confront someone. Arguments are just not my thing. Second, I guess that I was quite gullible (or blind), because it was literally nearly ten years before the penny finally dropped for me and I realised that *I* should have been finding bills to pay too, and stashing the money away for the time when I would end up being a single mum on the pension needing every cent I could scrape together. If only I'd had *that* thought all those years earlier! Facepalm.

No Judgement. No condemnation. Just acceptance.

The most blatant bit of chicanery though came just around the time that our youngest child was born and the joint account was suddenly cleaned out and overdrawn. I phoned up the bank to talk to someone about it and ask some questions. Prior to that conversation I actually had no idea that we were even able to organise an overdraft on the account, so I wanted to know how it had been able to happen. The very helpful man at the bank told me that the overdraft facility was indeed there in the background, but that it could only have been specifically activated by one of the signatories to the joint account. When I then asked my hubby about this, he was quite surprised! He said he knew nothing about it! He had no idea at all how we could have possibly ended up with an overdraft! How on earth could that have happened? There were only two of us holding the account, and I knew full well it wasn't me who had arranged for the overdraft, so I didn't have to be Sherlock Holmes to figure out who the mystery person was.

I used to think that he just lied to cover up his gambling, and sometimes I think he just did it for the hell of it, or maybe it was a habit? It wasn't until a year or so after he'd actually left us that I realised that he actually *believed* (at least some of) the crap that he was coming up with! I have a vivid memory of waiting on a platform for my train to arrive while being harangued over the phone about him wanting to put our youngest into day care for an extra day a week. His argument was that he wanted to be able to pick her up from the daycare centre, rather than having to collect her in person from me. I had a couple of objections to this plan. First because he said that he would pay for the extra day (Ha! Ha! Like that would *ever* happen!) and because the weekday that he chose was our Mother's Group meet up day, when both she and I could catch up with the other mums and the bubs she was growing up with. I remember saying something along the lines of not wanting to have her in day care for an extra day. Rather surprisingly he sort of agreed with this point of view and then said that he didn't want her in day care for five days a week like her older sibling had been. Well slice me and dice me and fry me in butter! I was absolutely floored! He dead set believed that her brother had been in day care five days a week and he didn't think that this was a good thing! Not only was his memory just plain wrong (it was two, sometimes three days a week), his argument clearly showed that he had absolutely *no* clue as to how day care fees were even scaled! Considering I only worked part-time two days a week when I came back from maternity leave, there was no way on God's earth that I could *ever* have been able to afford to pay for five days of day care! Boy! Was that little episode an eye opener for me!

Do these compulsive liars have a 'tell'? In other words, do they have a behaviour or gesture that gives them away? After a long time I think I figured out what my partner's 'tell' was, though I'm not going to mention it here! I don't want my secret blown. A friend who was also married to a compulsive gambler used to face the same problem of her husband lying. In fact, she said that one time he came out with an obvious lie about something completely unrelated to gambling, and then dobbed himself in by saying "I don't know why I even said that!" Go figure! This guy certainly had a 'tell' though. Whenever he started up gambling again he'd be chugging down antacid like it was the nectar of the gods, and off would go the alarm bells for her. Ding! Ding! Ding! Do you know anyone a little too keen on the old antacids?

It's probably worth keeping in mind that you are not going to be the only one that your gambler lies to. As well as their family members, they may also lie to their counsellor (if they have one) to hide the extent of their gambling. Their deceit may also extend to concealing illegal behaviours such as forgery, fraud, theft or embezzlement that they may engage in to get hold of money to gamble with.

What Makes A Good Liar?

> <u>Lie</u>: *a false statement made with deliberate intent to deceive; an intentional untruth.*

According to an interesting article I read on detecting lies and deceit (Vrij, "Good liars" Sci Am 2008, 378-381), good liars are people whose natural behaviour disarms suspicion. My partner was a very friendly, chatty, charming type. He certainly didn't come across (to me anyway) as a dodgy, sneaky, dishonest sort of character. They also don't find it mentally difficult to lie, and they don't experience the usual sorts of emotions that most of us would feel if we lied, such as feelings of guilt, fear or even a bit of pleasure at hoodwinking someone. To them it is totally commonplace and unexceptional.

Good liars tend to be natural performers and good actors, and they are able to think on their feet and give an answer without having to wait too long and arouse suspicion. A bit like the Sir Humphrey Appleby character in 'Yes Minister', liars seem to be able to come up with a convincing and credible answer to almost everything, though the response might be vague and long winded and actually completely evade the question that was being asked. Good liars also have a good memory. They've got to remember to keep their story straight, after all. Another gift of the good liar is that they have excellent decoding skills and can read people like a book. My partner had the freaky ability to nail people in mere seconds after meeting them, to the extent that he could nail down the type of car they would be likely to drive and the suburb where they lived. I used to think it was a skill that was a bit like hypnosis – it could be used for both good or evil, depending on how the power was wielded.

Common Lies From The Playbook Of The Compulsive Gambler/Liar

You could maybe have a bit of fun and turn this section into a sensible drinking game. You know the type – brew a nice cup of tea then watch an episode of Outlander and have a sip every time Jamie says "Sassenach." You get the drift.

I think that what we have with gamblers is a mix of outright lies that bear no relationship with reality, part-lies that just might have an element of truth to them (just enough to make you doubt yourself), and the lies which fall into the bucket called 'deliberately distorted facts'. Having done this for some time and perfected their art, liars get so good at lying that they could probably do it in their sleep. If you're in doubt about the veracity of what you're being told by someone, my advice would definitely be to take it all with a grain of salt, and watch what they *do*, not what they *say*.

The following are a selection of some of the 'best' lies that I've heard. No doubt you've heard plenty of your own, but see how many ring a bell with you. First one to get a full card and yell "Bingo!" wins. Or loses, depending on how you look at it of course.

- *"I don't have a gambling problem."* Yes, that's right, *I* was the one with the problem, because *I* was the one who was worried about it. I think this is either a flat out lie or screaming denial. But then again I wonder, can you *really* lie to yourself that much and actually believe it? A study by Lorenz and Yaffee found that 81% of GA members reported hiding their gambling from their spouses. Surprise, surprise.

- *"I haven't been gambling with the money from the joint account/company account"* (fill in the blank). When there are only two of you with access to an account, this one seems pointless beyond measure.

- *"I invested the money in Scheme X, which has gone bust."* I'll never know if this one was true or not. This old chestnut falls into the category also known as *"you wouldn't believe what happened!"* Yep, you're right. I don't.

- *"My best friend was in trouble with the tax office and needed X thousands of dollars."* Said friend worked on oil rigs and so would have been raking in the dollars pretty nicely thank you very much. Or so I would have thought. It was also declared to be quite impossible to ask this friend to return *any* of the money. You just don't do that kind of thing to your friends who've borrowed staggeringly large chunks of money from you. It seems that a friend in dire need is a fairly commonly used ploy. Watch out for this one. Early on in the relationship, there was also the story of the former debt he had to pay off because he paid to have central heating put in a house he was renting with a former girlfriend. Yes, I know what you're thinking! If only I'd thought it too!

- *"Trust me, it'll be fine."* Trust? Trust? Who is this bunyip called 'Trust' and where do I find him? Whenever I heard this one it reminded me of Dame Edith Evans playing the part of Lady Bracknell in "The Importance of Being Earnest." She was referring to ignorance rather than trust, but I think the end result is the same: it's "like a delicate exotic fruit; touch it and the bloom is gone." Gone, gone, gone. When you can no longer trust someone that you believe you should have been able to trust it leaves you feeling terribly, terribly lost, doesn't it?

PART III
Care of the Concerned Significant Other

"Most of the early problems with this unit were due to an inadequate instruction book, translated from the German into English by someone illiterate in both languages."

—Bulletin of the Washington Society of Cinematographers,
November 1967

FIVE

Killling Your Puppy

A FEW YEARS ago I was part of a team taking part in a course designed to help researchers commercialise their work, with the hope of reaping some tasty financial rewards for all their years of hard work. The first task we were all set was to go off and interview at least one hundred people who we thought were our target clients. The idea was to find out if there actually was a need for your particular widget. If the need did exist, we then had to find out how much were people willing to pay for it. We had a couple of facilitators for these sessions, and one of them had a bit of an accent. He could have been Dutch, though I'm not completely sure. I can still hear his voice though, telling us we had to see if we would need to 'kill our puppy'. I think it was a combination of his accent and the way he said it, but it's a phrase that's stuck in my mind like a sound worm ever since. The 'puppy' was the invention (or life's work) that had already taken so much time and effort for the researchers to bring to the table. If it turned out that our customers didn't see a need for it, weren't interested, or couldn't afford it, then your 'puppy' would have to be killed. The point being, that although it would be gut-wrenching to end up with this result, at least you got the bad news early on and so didn't then keep pouring more time, more energy and more money into an idea that was going nowhere, no matter how much you'd hoped and dreamed otherwise.

So this is where the title of this chapter "Killing the puppy" comes from. In the case of people like you and I, the puppy is the idea that living with a compulsive gambler could ever realistically end up as a 'happily ever after' story. We need to seriously examine the idea, hope or dream that how we think things should work out when you are married to a gambler, is how they are actually likely to work out when we look at them in the cold hard light of day. If you went out and asked a hundred people if they thought living with a compulsive gambler was a good idea and was likely to end well for all concerned, how do you think they would respond? If you look at it as starkly as that, do you think *anyone* would say 'yes'?

This is really hard-hitting stuff and is likely to be very confronting for you, though I'd hazard a guess that it's not the first time you've asked yourself if you're really happy doing what you're doing. It's probably fair to say that if you're reading this book then you aren't at ease with the situation you are in. Whatever decisions you make, remember that it has to feel right for you. What suits one person may not suit another. I didn't end up leaving my partner, but plenty of other women do. Each person's journey is their own, so I take an absolute position of making no judgements about other people's decisions.

Be fair, be kind, be true to yourself.

One of the most insulting things we can do to a fellow human being is to confront their core values. This is why they say you should never talk about religion or politics at dinner parties. Ideals and beliefs are like the foundation stones of our lives. Plenty of us grew up in homes where a particular religion was important to the family unit, or a particular political ideology may have been held up above all the others. When you are old enough to challenge the beliefs that you soaked up subconsciously while young, you instinctively know that it may be a good idea to keep any new ideas of your own to yourself at times, so as not to rock the family boat unnecessarily.

If your core values around money are poles apart from your partner's, then that's bound to cause some tension. In my own case my partner spent money faster than I could earn it, he spent borrowed money, and if he had any money at all in his pocket he had to spend it. On the other hand, I had grown up having to keep a close eye on the pennies and so actually manage my money well. I like saving and seeing my money grow, because to me that gives me a feeling of security and safety. What he did with money had my stomach tied up in knots, whereas he probably saw my attempts at saving as simply hoarding good gambling money. Clearly we were never going to be singing from the same page of the money hymn book.

The sales books all tell us that we buy things with our emotions and then defend that decision with logic. If you've gone in a bit deep to buy that shiny new car with all the bells and whistles, then you will come up with a string of good reasons to back up the purchase. It's a new car, therefore it's safer to travel in. It's got better fuel economy, so you won't be so much of an environmental bandit when you're driving around in it. It comes with roadside assist, so all will be well if it 'fails to proceed' somewhere a long way from home. The stereo is really good, and anyway, who still has a car with a tape deck these days? You see other people driving the same new car, so that means if other people are doing it, we must have made the right decision. Every time we see something that confirms what we believe, our bodies give us a nice dopamine rush, to reinforce our decisions no matter how tenuously they were made.

Your Own Journey To Your Own Holy Grail

Do you remember that part of Indiana Jones and the Last Crusade when Indiana takes his leap of faith from the lion's head and is able to cross over the chasm to the where the Templar knight on the other side is guarding the holy grail? In real life you can't just get from the lion's den straight to the holy grail of a new serenity and security in one jump. The job at hand is to work your way through all the steps from anxiety and fear until you reach acceptance on the other side and are moving forward. It might be a much slower journey, but you'll learn a lot about yourself along the way. I've popped the diagram below in here so that you can get a sense of where you're at right now. It's based on the change curve by Elizabeth Kubler-Ross.

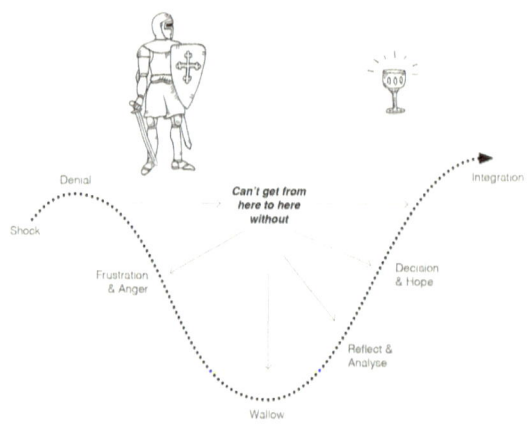

What Might You Be Feeling?

Coming to terms with the fact that you've hitched your wagon to a compulsive gambler is not likely to leave you feeling good about the situation. Assuming that most of us don't know that the new love of our life has a gambling problem when we hitch our wagon to their train, we make plans and develop expectations for our future that can come crashing down around our ears when reality hits. When we've expected a certain outcome and it doesn't eventuate, we can be left feeling frustrated and disappointed. We can also become anxious because we quite rightly expect the whole gambling thing to have a negative outcome for us for the foreseeable future. In fact the stark reality of the here and now is usually a place where very real negative experiences leave us feeling fearful about what's going to happen next. The key piece of advice I want to give to you now is to be fair, be kind, and be true to yourself.

These are all quite a contrast to the feelings of relief that that came some time after my partner left. Don't get me wrong about this - having your world turned upside down causes a whole lot of distress, but it's a very reassuring feeling when you know that now you're the only one taking money out of the bank account. You can be confident that you're not going to get any nasty surprises when you go to pay for the groceries. There's a great feeling of relaxation and an absence of anxiety when the phone rings or you get a text message and you just know that it's not going to be anyone chasing you for money, or it's not going to be the bank telling you your account is overdrawn again. It's a really lovely feeling of relief when all that particular unpleasantness stops.

It can be hard though, to admit it when we're wrong. There's all that time that you've invested in the relationship, all the emotion and the effort spent building your life as a couple. I've read somewhere that the more people that come to your wedding, the more likely you are to stay together for longer. We don't want to look silly in front of all our friends and relatives do we? We make plans for how we think our life will turn out. When someone other than us changes those plans we don't like it. You're bound to feel a bit out of control. Then there are all the emotions that you'll likely be feeling and working your way through such as shock, anger, anxiety, confusion, overwhelm, denial, guilt and sadness.

Be fair, be kind, be true to yourself.

The fact of the matter is that people resist change if the change is forced upon them. Whereas if the change comes from the inside it's more likely to be successful and lasting. What I realised when I was reading something from Alan Deutch's book *Change or Die*, is that one of the reasons we unconsciously resist change is that actually making a change can invalidate all the previous years of our earlier behaviour. For example, if you lost a large amount of weight and became slim and fit, then why did you spend so many of your prime years being obese? Sometimes what stops us from making a change is that we're not able to re-write our life story.

There's also likely to be some anxiety about the future for you to work through as well. You might be asking yourself just how much money am I going to have to find to cover the bills and feed the kids. How much is my workload going to have to increase to manage all this? How will I find the time to try and keep this house of cards together so that it doesn't collapse in a messy pile?

There's bound to be some trepidation and dread around the situation, whether you choose to leave or to stay. As well as uncertainty about the outcome in terms of how will *he* react? There's also the question of how will *I* react? Not to mention the fact that if you leave, you can see exactly what you are going to lose. But you can't see what we might gain in the future. It is a leap of faith because what you stand to lose is real, while what you stand to gain is intangible.

I love the quote below from Ralph Waldo Trine's book *In tune with the Infinite*:

> *"If in any way we try to live to suit others we never shall suit them, and the more we try the more unreasonable and exacting do they become. The government of your life is a matter that lies entirely between God and yourself, and when your life is swayed and influenced from any other source you are on the wrong path."*

Pack Shot vs Product Shot

Finding yourself married to a compulsive gambler is a classic story of unmet expectations. You know how this plays out. You buy a frozen meal from the supermarket because the picture on the outside of the packet looks really tasty. So you pay for it, take it home and get it out of the wrapper, only to find that it doesn't look nearly as appetising as you were lead to believe by the image on the box. And therein lies the problem. What do *you* think you were lead to believe when you started on your journey with your bright shiny compulsive gambler? Did you cook up your own ideas of a wonderful future without paying enough attention to the raw ingredients that you had to work with? Or did you think to yourself "Well, I know the crusts are a bit mouldy, but if I cut those off and toast it then cover it with jam and it'll be fine," while the little voice in your head is reassuring you that "A bit of mould won't *kill* you, will it?" These little 'lies' we tell ourselves are a defence mechanism.

Soren Kirkegaard made a lot of sense when he said that *"There are two ways to be fooled. One is to believe what isn't true. The other is to refuse to accept what is true."*

Chances are that you might try and tell yourself that you don't know what to do, but deep down you know that you do.

Be fair, be kind, be true to yourself.

As Leland Val Van de Wall wisely said, *"The degree to which a person can grow is directly proportional to the amount of truth that he can accept about himself without running away."*

And boy, did I want to run!

Funeral For A Marriage

The following are some of the questions that I was asked to submit written answers for when I applied to the Catholic Church for an annulment of my marriage to the problem gambler. I have to say that this was an incredibly eye opening experience. It took many hours to write out the whole statement and answer all of the questions, but for me it was well worth doing and it was quite startling to see in black and white the answers I'd written down. When you physically hold in your hands your own written history of the relationship where you've detailed all the ways in which it went pear-shaped, you find it much harder to wriggle away from the truth.

When the misgivings are just airy fairy thoughts in your head I guess there's a chance that they aren't real. The beauty of this exercise is that when the ink hits the paper it becomes very, very real and it forces you to take ownership of that reality. I remember reading over it all once I'd finished, and saying "I did *what?* Gosh, I *did* do that!" I really don't know why it came as such a shock to me. I had lived it after all. Maybe up until that point I'd felt that I could tell myself a different story and get away with it. Not anymore.

So I'd like to invite you to take a reality check on your own situation now by grabbing a pen and paper and working your way through the following questions. Don't rush through this. Take your time and really think about each of the questions. As Polonius said to Laertes in Hamlet: "This above all: to thine own self be true." You might just surprise yourself.

- What is the background of your partner – economic circumstances growing up, education, occupations of family members, whether the house was a happy one, nature of relationships between family members, particular lifestyle of family, and special problems that may have existed. If you do the same for yourself you might see a contrast between you emerging.

- What was his or her character before you partnered up with them. Give incidents or important events. Include details of their personality and temperament; attractive/unattractive characteristics; preferred social activities and interests; any significant previous relationships; plans or ambitions for the future; capacity to handle money, responsibility, alcohol, drugs? What did your former partner regard as important in life?

- Courtship. Indicate how you met your partner, and how long and well you got to know one another before you partnered up. Was the relationship ever broken off? Was the courtship unusual in any way?

- Wedding and reception (if there was one) – who made the arrangements and who met the expenses? Did anything unusual occur around the time of the event and was the day a happy one for both parties?

- Story of the partnership. Give examples of incidents or important events that have taken place. Include details of the honeymoon, places and dates of residence, types and periods of employment, birth of children, financial arrangements, quality of communication, quality of the sexual relationship, social activities, any interference from outside parties, any health problems, special difficulties, any professional help received. Why did the partnership break down?

- Story since the partnership began. Include details or present circumstances of both; custody, access and maintenance arrangements since the partnership broke down.

I've deleted the next question that was included in my own case because it is specific to people who are applying for an annulment, and I know that most people won't be going through that process. The question was about my partner's attitude to my application for an annulment. Considering that he didn't have a religious bone in his body, I didn't think he'd give two hoots. But it turned out that I was wrong about that too. Apparently, the people who do raise objections tend to do so because they are either controlling, or they want to cause problems for their ex. Can you tick either of those boxes? As the lovely Louise Hay used to say, the only people who get upset about you setting boundaries are the ones who were benefitting from you having none.

Risk Analysis Or Predicting The Future?

Financial advisors and your superannuation company will ask you a string of questions to find out what your appetite for risk is when you are looking at options for investing your money. This is so that they can then point you in the right direction of the types of investments that you're most likely to be comfortable with.

Those of you who have already parted company with their compulsive gambler have already assessed the risk to your present and future selves, and decided that staying put was odds on to end up extremely badly for you.

I can remember asking a gambling counsellor something along the lines of whether I was really stupid for staying in the relationship. His reply really pulled me up short. This guy didn't sugar coat anything, and really hit the nail on the head when he told me that staying with my husband obviously filled a need that I had. Ouch! That made me sit up and take notice! I really hadn't looked at it from that perspective before, but although my initial internal response was to resist that idea, I had to admit later on that he was actually right. In hindsight I could see that on the one hand I was thinking that the nice green paddock out there would be great to run around in, but on the other hand I had become so acclimatised to the four walls of the stable that we shut ourselves into day after day. At least in the stable someone will come and see you every day. If you end up on the outside you may have to start fending for yourself.

What I'm getting at here is that I know how scary the idea of upsetting the apple cart can be, and I also know that getting as clear as possible about the options that we have can be very helpful, so what I want you to do now is consider your circumstances in a structured way. Making a decision about what to do about the position you're in, is one of those times when it will be incredibly helpful to see things in black and white. Just grabbing a pen and paper and catching the thoughts that are whirling around in your head and nailing them down on paper could help to give you the clarity you need to make a decision about whether to maintain the status quo, or pack your bags and go.

So, if like me, you haven't left (and whether you do or not, that decision is entirely for you to make), then realistically would you agree that it's a good idea to at least give some time to identify the pros and cons of staying or leaving so that you can take a reality check?

If we're looking at the chances of your partner continuing to gamble, would you say that they were rare? Unlikely? Possible? Given that you're reading this book, I'd say it's a fair bet to run with the premise that you'd honestly rate it as either likely or almost certain – would you agree?

OK then, if we're agreed that continued gambling and throwing away hard earned money is in the range of 'likely' to 'dead set certainty', then our next step is to weigh up the consequences of that. So, if we're now really quite sure that this ongoing gambling thing is a done deal, what are the likely negative consequences for you if you hang around to see how the last race is going to pan out? This is where you need to consider what you are comfortable with risking, and therefore comfortable with losing. Even though you're not the one who is gambling, you'll still be suffering from what is known as Sexually Transmitted Debt.

First up, should we consider the financial risk? How much money has this arrangement already cost you? If it's fair to say that increasing debts that are likely compounded with a good solid credit card interest rate would scare the absolute hell out of you, write that down. How much are you prepared to keep shelling out to keep your head above water? Is it a percentage of your income? 10%? 20%? More? Is it a dollar amount? "I'm prepared to see $20K, 50K etc go round the s-bend each year". How long do you think can you keep that up? Think about your own earning capacity. How close are you to retirement? Do you have any health issues that might slow your earning capacity down a bit – or a lot? If you have a mortgage, would you say the chances of losing your home were so-so, high or "I can see the bailiff coming down the driveway"? How does that *feel* to you when you think about it? Personally, the idea of retiring to a cardboard box under a bridge at the ripe old age of 70 was pretty damn scary and used to really freak me out!

How about we look at your health a bit more closely. Has your partner's gambling affected your physical health? You're well acquainted with the fact that it's got an emotional and psychological impact on you, but are there other things as well? Loss of sleep, stomach upsets, headaches? Can you see yourself making lifelong friends with these consequences of another's actions, or do you feel more of the type of reaction we all get when you're in the supermarket and hear one of those poxed-up kids with that awful wet sounding cough that reverberates around the aisles and just makes you want to get the hell out of there before you catch something nasty?

Have you thought about the intangible things that you really can't put a dollar value on? Your reputation for example. If you're forever covering up for them with family and friends and bailing them out, is that likely to compromise you in any way? Do you have a business that could be negatively effected. Is your name on any joint contracts? If they are splashing around in a sea of fraud or other illegal activities to fund their habit, or even paddling around at the edges getting their toes wet, what effect is that likely to have on you if a huge wave comes along and swamps them? Could you be caught in a rip along with them? Are there legal ramifications for you that might come as part of the deal? Do you really want to find out the hard way what "joint and several" means on a contract? I did, and my heartfelt advice is make sure you know exactly what this term means BEFORE you sign a contract with their name and yours on it, because it means that if they do a runner, you will be stuck with the debt.

Even if the shadowy world of dodgy dealings isn't their gig – yet – what about your own plans for the future? How do you see your *own* retirement? Are you definitely having that bucket list cruise on the Queen Mary 2, or tootling around the countryside in a caravan with all the other grey nomads, or are you seeing yourself missing out on the rewards that you'd planned for yourself in order to just keep yourself afloat? Will it be an old age of baked beans or beef bourguignon? If things stay as they are, will you be able to retire when you'd planned to, or might you be facing working for longer in a workforce where older employees may not be the most sought after candidate for the job?

Write it all down and then read it back to yourself, preferably out loud so that you can hear yourself telling yourself what you *really* think. Was it as scary as a Stephen King horror story? If you wouldn't read that stuff to your kids before they go to bed, why do it to yourself?

"Smithers had thwarted my earlier attempt to take candy from a baby, but with him out of the picture, I was free to wallow in my own crapulence."

—Monty Burns

SIX

Overwhelm And Victimhood

THE WAY I'm using the idea of 'wallowing in your crapulence' is as a proxy for victimhood. So let me ask you right now, are you wallowing in the crapulence of your 'victim' story? What is the emotional and physical environment that you choose to set yourself in? Hopefully by the end of this book, you'll see that you have some very good reasons to NOT wallow in your own crapulence. While allowing yourself recovery time after stress is very important, you need to ask yourself if you are staying in the cocoon because you're rejuvenating and evolving, or are you using it as an excuse to not come back out into the open. If you are honest with yourself, you know the answer to that one - even if you don't want to admit it.

The victim story is just great though isn't it? We can get to be a bit of a martyr (if that's your gig), and we get to be special. The payoff is that we get sympathy from family and friends, etc, etc. Do you feel a bit self-righteous? Do you feel you deserve more? And are you asking "Why is this happening to me?" Maybe the question you should be asking is why shouldn't it be happening to you. Everyone has crapulence to deal with in life. No one is exempt. If you feel like you're getting something from the 'pity party', ask yourself if it is supportive of your spirit in any way whatsoever? It might feel that staying in your pain is a problem that you can feel comfortable with, but I want you to shine a light on what's really going on if there's any chance that you are using this problem as an excuse to avoid moving forward with your life. Being sad and miserable all the time is not only taking a toll on you emotionally. It is also taking a toll on you physically as well as spiritually.

What this means is that wallowing in your crapulence can be a real drain on your immune system and make you more prone to illness. I'm sure you know someone who says "I always catch a cold every winter." I don't doubt that it's true because that's the story that they've told themselves. It literally becomes a self-fulfilling prophecy for them. If you're still identifying yourself as the victim of a gambler, then you're still letting them have power over you. The kicker is that it's not the gambler who is taking your power away from you. So I want to ask you are you like the chalk in the glass of ink in the old t.v. ads featuring Mrs Marsh and her magic Colgate toothpaste? Do you remember the kiddies standing around her looking surprised and cooing "Oooh, it does get in!" when she snapped the chalk to show them how far the ink had soaked in to the chalk? Don't be like Mrs Marsh's chalk. Don't let the bad stuff soak in.

Be fair, be kind, be true to yourself.

Do you think it might be better to tell yourself good things and surround yourself with happy people? Rather than join 'support' groups made up of people who whinge and moan and reinforce the 'woe is me' story of the other members? Do you think it might be better to instead join what Caroline Myss refers to as 'resource' groups, where people come together with ideas and stories to share to help each other. "I tried 'X' and it worked for me", "This is how I did 'Y', maybe that would work for you as well?" Can you see the difference when you look at things from the point of view of potential solutions?

Affirmations are great for helping you change your perspective and outlook. We'll look into them in detail a little later on. What I want you to see right now is that no matter how bad a situation may seem, there is always something that can make it at least a little better. Sometimes we do have to be brutally honest with ourselves though, and be prepared for it to be a bit uncomfortable when we take account of where our negative thoughts and self-talk have taken us. The situation may seem overwhelming, but is it as bad as you really think? The seasons change year in and year out. Nothing stays the same. Everything goes in cycles and life continually changes. Spring always follows winter, day always follows night. And so it is with the seasons of your life.

Be fair, be kind, be true to yourself

Your Bowl Isn't Empty

What I'm sharing with you here is a perspective to get you out of your crapulence. If you've ever had a cat, or know anyone with a cat, you may have come across the 'My bowl is empty' type of cat. My family share our home with one of these. Barry is a lovely ginger cat adopted from the local pound. Aside from shredding the lounge, he's a pretty awesome family member. One of his other bad habits though (and this is common to many cats) is his unfortunate and severe 'domestic blindness' when it comes to his food bowl. If there are still biscuits around the edge of the bowl, but he can see the bottom of the bowl, he starts carrying on as if his bowl is completely empty! OMG! Much cat whinging and whining and haranguing of the humans in the house ensues. If whinging was an Olympic sport, he could whinge for England. It turns out though, that it's remarkably easy to fix Barry's problem. Just a shake or a tap of the bowl gets the biscuits from the edge back into the middle of the bowl and hoorah! We've performed the 'Miracle of the Biscuits'! The once barren bowl is now seemingly bountifully supplied with biscuits again, and now he can't whinge because he's too busy eating. The biscuits at the edge were always there. The ones back in the middle are the same ones that he always had access to, but either couldn't see them, or didn't want to see them. The point I'm making here is that from Barry's point of view it was easier for him to sound like he was starving and have someone else fix his problem for him, rather than having to put the effort in and get the dang biscuits for himself.

Life is often like Barry's biscuit bowl. The same opportunities and good things that I started experiencing once I'd gotten out of the trap I was in, were out there for me when I was in the trap, it's just that I couldn't see them at the time. All I could see was what I *didn't* have. If we keep telling ourselves that we don't have the resources, time, money, energy, whatever, then we likely won't be able to see opportunities to get what we want out of life. To literally turn your life around, all you have to do is stop whinging and start making an effort to help yourself. If you do, before too long you'll see that the rewards are absolutely out there.

Be fair. Be kind. Be true to yourself.

So now that we've had a look at the importance of the internal environment we set up via our thoughts, it's time to move on to the next part of the crapulence story which is all about the importance of the external environment. What do you surround yourself with? What have you got around you that makes you feel happy and good within yourself? Or sad and miserable? Bruce Lipton wrote some awesome stuff on the importance of our environment in his book *The biology of belief*. The point is that we just can't flourish if we're in a crappy environment. Are you drowning in 'stuff'? Do you feel 'stuck' in your life? Are you holding onto things that aren't really necessary to keep around you anymore? Space clearing and decluttering apparently works well if you do it in Autumn as well as in Spring. The idea is that you do it at the beginning and near the end of a cycle (Winter being the end).

It's time to get real with yourself and come clean if you are carrying your crap around with you. In my council area, they collect your garbage once a week. As long as you (or the kids) remember to put the bin out, that stuff's gone! We don't hang onto it and make an art installation out it.

Be fair, be kind, be true to yourself.

It doesn't really matter what you have or don't have, the spaces where you choose to spend most of your time can be orderly and uncluttered. Louise Hay has a lovely affirmation about loving your home and putting love in every corner. Make your home and your workplace pleasant places for you to be. How long do you want to spend your life being somewhere that makes you feel physically uncomfortable? Rather than living from the stinky bog at the bottom of the valley where your world is hemmed in and you can't see past your nose, live from the top of the mountain where the air is clean and clear and you have the freedom of being able to see for miles.

You may not have thought about the importance of your environment, but it's important to appreciate that it does have a very real effect on you and how you feel. Casinos certainly believe in the effect it has on their punters – think about the absence of clocks, and the garish carpets which make you look up at the flashing lights rather than down at the floor. Supermarkets do too. There's a lot of science behind where the corn flakes are stacked and what kind of background music is playing. Does where you live support you? If you are still living with your gambler, do you have a place away from home that you can escape to and clear your head and renew yourself? Forest bathing is all the rage at the moment, so do you like to walk in the bush and talk to trees? Or do you prefer to sit on the beach and listen to the waves rolling in? The places that support your spirit are good places to spend your time.

How do you see your environment and surroundings supporting you in the future? I can remember many discussions with my ex about money and the ever growing mortgage, and in my mind I could absolutely, dead set see myself being 70 years old and the two of us living in a cardboard box under a bridge somewhere! Not a great image of the future to be holding in your mind!

If you happen to be on your own now, how much of your shared belongings (with their old energy) do you have still surrounding you? Are there curtains you've always hated? If you're looking at them every day of your life and you don't even like them, then get rid of them. If it's just not financially feasible at this stage to replace big items such as furniture, maybe you could change the 'feeling' of them with a quick coat of paint. That dark old bookcase you never really liked might look completely different if it was spray painted duck egg blue. Change the old energy and freshen things up that surround you.

Talking of colour, the effect of colours is an interesting area to read up on. Take pink for example. 'Drunk tank pink' or 'prison pink' are used to settle fractious people down. Fast food 'restaurants' tend to use warm colours like red, orange and yellow to make you want to eat more. Royal blue is the colour recommended if you're wanting to feel more powerful. As the name suggests, it is a colour that used to be worn by kings and its effect was to project an image of power.

To make yourself feel more powerful you need to feel safe and protected. The advice from the Feng Shui experts is to find the power position when you enter in a room and take that. The power position is a place that faces the entrance of a room and has a solid wall behind you. High backed chairs are good, as you need to feel protected from behind. Do you remember Victoria Grayson's wonderful high backed chair from the tv series Revenge? That chair was awesome! Everybody wanted a chair like that! The chair had nearly as many fans as the show did. Maybe you deserve a chair like that, after all, if you think about it, you don't see too many powerful people portrayed sitting perched uncomfortably on a kitchen stool.

Be fair, be kind, be true to yourself.

If you don't like where you are, and you are free to move – then move. Remember, you are not a tree! I myself am not a huge fan of cold weather. I can remember watching movies set in some God-forsaken, arctic wind-blasted town where the people would walk around looking like the Michelin Man because they'd be wearing at least six layers of clothing, and looking downright miserable while they did it. The factory was always closing down and the town football team were on the skids, and I would just think to myself "Why on earth would anybody *choose* to live in a place like that? If life was so crappy, why not move somewhere else? I couldn't see why anyone would actually choose to live in those frozen waste lands in the first place. Again though, I suppose the environment that suits one person would not suit another. One time I was on a train in Sydney and there was a group of Greek girls talking about how they didn't like the Australian coast because it was too 'open'. It seems that in Greece you can see other islands from the shore of your own island, and they didn't like not being able to see the lights from other islands when they were on an Australian beach. There was just too much clear ocean for them. From my point of view, I had precisely the opposite opinion. I would feel hemmed in if I wasn't able to see uninterrupted water when I gazed out to sea. Horses for courses.

Talking of feeling crowded, do you share a landline with your gambler so that people chasing them for money can phone you and harangue you in your own home? Landlines are becoming less common these days, but someone I know tells of a vivid memory of answering the home phone one Sunday morning and being grilled by someone from some bank looking for her husband because he owed them money and wasn't paying. Unfortunately for her, that Sunday was the day their youngest was to be christened, so she had house guests, one of which was her mother - and she was standing right next to her during the conversation! Awkward! Hubby was out doing some 'work' with a 'friend', so sadly she couldn't pass the phone over to him at the time. These days I don't have a landline, but even if I did, I'm tolerably certain that I wouldn't be needing to field those kinds of phone calls! Whether it's your landline or your mobile, it's so nice to be able to hear a phone ring and not be thinking, "Oh God! Is that someone chasing us for money?"

If your gambler is doing illegal stuff and that's not your gig, do you think you'd feel more comfortable if you didn't have to wonder if you'd be answering the front door to the police the next time the doorbell rang? Remember, as we said earlier, you are not a tree. You don't have to stay rooted to whatever spot you find yourself in.

How do you know if you've kicked the victim habit and moved on from your story? According to Gregg Braden, if you no longer feel any charge when you tell it, you've moved on past it. This book is all about getting you to the point where your story has no 'charge' anymore.

Be fair. Be kind. Be true to yourself.

"The weak can never forgive.
Forgiveness is the attribute of the strong."

–Mahatma Ghandi

SEVEN

Forgiveness

DEPENDING on what point you've reached in your journey with your gambler, you may either find this chapter helpful, or challenging, or possibly both. Or you may feel that you want to skip it altogether just at present.

The Other "F" Word – Forgiveness

Whatever you feel now is right for you, and that's just fine. Be compassionate with yourself. Take time if you need to. It will still be here when you feel ready to come back and sit with it again.

No Judgement. No condemnation. Just acceptance.

People have written whole books on the subject of forgiveness. I know, because I've read quite a few of them. The basic messages are roughly the same, although different authors approach the topic from different angles, which means that you can get quite a number of different viewpoints on the ins and outs of it. I'll introduce you to some resources that I've found incredibly helpful, though I appreciate that what resonates with me may not resonate with you in your own particular circumstances. If any of these resources don't work for you, just move on to another one and see how that goes. I've certainly had books recommended to me by friends who've absolutely loved them and found them a great help, but I've just not been able to get into them at all. As I said, a lot of them are all saying basically the same thing, but you may have to look into a few to find one or more that you particularly click with.

As Louise Hay said, "forgiveness is a gift that you give to yourself". I know from first hand experience that forgiving someone who you perceive to have wronged you, does indeed set you free. All the great teachers seem to want us to realise that by forgiving someone who we see as having wronged us, we are not condoning their actions or conferring approval on what they did, but that what we are doing by working through our feelings of anger, hurt, humiliation, sadness, etc, etc, is moving towards the other side of forgiveness, so that we can reclaim our power. By choosing to stay standing in the feeling that someone else has wronged you, you hand over responsibility for your feelings and emotions to another person. Taking responsibility for your own part in what has happened to you means that you are able to take back your power. This in turn means that you can change your present situation, and therefore your future.

Stuart Wilde used to say that all anger comes initially from an impending sense of loss or an actual loss. When you're feeling angry with your gambler, look for the loss – it's bound to be more than just a financial one. Try not to let the anger sit with you for too long though. Remember what we said about not wallowing.

Your partner may well have dragged you through a load of crap and they may have really wronged you, but if at the end of the day you are the only one worried about said crap, then you may as well get rid of the stink and move on.

I think it's important to remember that the gambler is not the only one you'll need to forgive. You'll probably need to put your own name up near the top of your 'People who did me wrong' list as well. After all, if you stayed in the dungheap for any length of time, you can't blame anyone else for it. That can be a hard reality to face up to I know, but beating yourself up about it is like sitting in the proverbial rocking chair in that it gives you something to do, which makes it feel like you're doing something while you're wallowing in all that self- pity, but at the end of the day it's really not getting you anywhere at all.

No Judgement. No condemnation. Just acceptance.

So, our plan moving forward is to pretend that we're the characters William Thacker and Anna Scott from that cracker of a movie *'Notting Hill'*. We have jumped the high spiky fence in the dark of night so that we can wander around the lovely garden of forgiveness for a while, lie on the cool grass and gaze up at the stars. Then we'll have a go at climbing out of our victim story in readiness for moving ahead to the next part of the journey. I've had so many absolutely brilliant experiences and met some incredibly awesome people since I put the life I had with my gambling ex-partner behind me, and I can see that all those wonderful things wouldn't have been able to happen if things had stayed the way they were. Don't look on your time with the gambler as 'wasted'. If you try to see that it has delivered some lessons that life was trying to teach you, you'll be in the position to take some learnings from the experiences you had. That way it's not such a stretch to consider that there *were* some positives to come out of it all. I think time spent on crappy intervals in your life is only really wasted if you learn nothing from what life was trying to show you. As lots of famous people have said, things don't happen *to* you, they happen *for* you.

Some of the books that I'd recommend are Colin Tipping's book *'Radical Forgiveness'*, *'Unconditional Forgiveness'* by Mary Hayes-Grieco, and Dr John DeMartini's *'Breakthrough Experience'*. Both Louise Hay and Wayne Dyer have also written a lot on this topic. These books are all different and will take you on the forgiveness journey in different ways, so hopefully you'll end up with an all-round experience by approaching the issue from different directions to get you back to the quiet, peaceful place at the centre of yourself.

The Radical Forgiveness Process

Colin Tipping's book *Radical Forgiveness* was one of the first books I read that was devoted to the process of forgiveness. It's quite an interesting read, though some of the concepts can be a little confronting if you've not come across them before. He differentiates what he calls Radical Forgiveness from 'traditional' forgiveness. Traditional forgiveness takes the view that something wrong has happened, and that there is someone to blame and be forgiven. Radical Forgiveness on the other hand takes the view that things aren't good or bad or right or wrong. It's just that we perceive them this way. And therefore, if nothing wrong has happened to us, we can't possibly be a victim.

Tipping's approach demystifies the spiritual concepts about the lessons we have come here to learn, and makes sense of the fact that we repeat patterns until we learn the lesson or heal the hurt that we've been put on the earth to do. He also explains that until we're ready to learn and heal we will seek out situations that will reflect back to us the experiences that we expect to have, in other words we experience things that will fit our 'story'. If you find this territory challenging, there is also a Radical Forgiveness CD that you can get to accompany the book. The CD takes you through the process which the book describes.

There is also a Radical Forgiveness worksheet that you can download and make your way through. I felt that it was a very good 'thinking' and 'feeling' exercise for me to do. It is designed to get you in touch with your emotions around a person or occurrence, and you then need to ask if you are *willing* to look at it from a different point of view. As you can probably tell by now, I think there is something quite cathartic about writing things down on paper and then reading back what you have written. The process starts with asking you to tell your story about what has upset you. You then move on to confronting (only on paper!) the person or event, being specific about what you blame them for, and then identify how that made you feel. You can then have a think about it all and decide whether or not you are willing or unwilling (or somewhere in between) to accept your feelings and not judge them. If you can own your feelings, then you may be willing to accept that no-one else can make you feel something because whatever you are feeling is just you reflecting to yourself how you need to see the situation.

The next step involves deciding if you are willing to recognise that you drew the situation to yourself in order to grow. Personally, I think you can't help but grow as a result of spending part of your life with a compulsive gambler. You then move on to examining your past to see if you can recognise any repeating patterns or coincidences. This is useful because it would indicate that you may have been presented with learning or healing opportunities in the past that you didn't see, or if you did see them then you didn't act on them.

The whole process draws to its conclusion by – hopefully - you realising that your victim story was the result of how you were interpreting the situation. You can then completely forgive yourself, and, if you feel that the energy around the person or situation has shifted since you began the worksheet, you write a note to them (just for yourself) that you forgive them, and accept them as they are, and can see the perfection in the situation.

It's quite a book, and quite a process. You may have to go over it a few times to get to a place where you are comfortable in yourself. And there are other ways of viewing and moving through the forgiveness process. If you feel you need to take a more physical approach to the job at hand, the next recommendation will be right up your street.

No Judgement. No condemnation. Just acceptance.

"Holding on to anger is like burning down your house in order to get rid of a rat."

−Swami Cidvilasananda

Unconditional Forgiveness

Unconditional Forgiveness is a book by Mary Hayes Greco. It is another brilliant gem that I have come across in my many rummagings through libraries and bookshops. As Molly Meldrum always used to say on Countdown, "Do yourself a favour" and get hold of this one. If you're after a physical process to work your way through forgiveness (rather than a mental one), this book really seems to hit that spot.

Mary was mentored for many years by Dr Edith Stauffe, a university professor and director of two counselling centres. Edith taught principles of unconditional love and forgiveness. Over time she observed that on the journey towards forgiveness there were certain tasks that needed to be performed, and certain milestones that people had to pass along the way before they reached their goal. Mary's eight Steps to Freedom are based on Edith's principles. Following the eight steps works the issue out of your system by dealing with whatever it is that you want to forgive on all levels of your being – physical, emotional, mental, energetic and spiritual. I found it to be a great process because I like to feel like I've really 'done something'.

As Mary says, pain is unavoidable, but suffering is optional. Absolutely no-one gets through life avoiding pain altogether, but you can make the decision to deal with the pain in such a way that it doesn't become suffering that goes on and on and on. She teaches that forgiveness is about releasing an expectation which *you* hold and which is causing you to suffer. We tend to expect people or situations to be a certain way, and our ego gets upset when things don't go the way we think is "right". Mary defines 'unconditional forgiveness' as a spiritual journey that is a profound transformational experience involving completely releasing any expectation that is causing us to suffer. The process brings us back to our natural state of wholeness and happiness which is independent of what others may have done, or may be presently doing. Depending on whether or not you are spiritual, she does refer to God in the book. If you have some reticence around the idea of God you could substitute this for whatever you perceive God or Higher Power to be. Mary also talks about energy and refers to the subtle energy system of the body such as the aura. She considers that it is the energy component of the eight Steps to Freedom which makes this method of forgiveness more genuinely renewing in a physical way, than many of the more intellectual approaches. It certainly is physical, I'll give her that!

I love that Mary talks about the fact that the process of forgiveness decreases stress within our body and improves our health because, as I've heard it said, "Your issues are in your tissues." She says that in 25 years of practicing and teaching forgiveness she found time after time a side effect of emotional healing was the resolution of a physical health problem that was rooted in the emotional issue. Louise Hay also talks about this in her book *You can heal your life*. Louise observed that sinus infections tended to start from irritation with someone close in the environment. Mary shares that she used to get a sinus infection about a week or so after being irritated by her husband about something. Interestingly, I also used to suffer quite a lot with sinusitis while I was living with my partner who gambled, but have been very pleasantly sinusitis free in the years since he left.

A very brief summary of Mary's eight Steps to Freedom now follows. Please be aware that this is just an overview! What follows is a bit like standing at ground level and looking at the edge of a crop circle in a paddock full of wheat. To really appreciate the Mandelbrot sets that the little green men have gone to what seems like an inordinate amount trouble to make for us to marvel at, you've got to get up higher so you can see intricacies of the whole thing. Likewise, to really appreciate what Mary is offering, you really should get hold of her book and work through these processes in detail for yourself.

What the eight steps are all about, is helping you to actually prepare for a change in your life.

1. State your will to make a change
2. Express your feelings exactly as they are inside you
3. Release expectations from your mind, one by one
4. Restore your boundaries
5. Open up to the Universe to get your needs met in a different way
6. Receive Spirit's healing energy into your personality
7. Send unconditional love to the other person and release him or her
8. See the good in the person or situation

Having worked your way through the eight steps, it's important to integrate your change and start living in a new way.

The exercise is addressing the fact that you have to be ready to want to change or you're not going to get the result you're after. For some people, holding on to their victimhood may give them a feeling of comfort, and they may not be ready for change just yet. If you're a person who doesn't like change in general, your attitude towards forgiveness as a life habit may mean that your progress in that direction is a bit like wading through a pool of treacle. Our paradigms like us to keep things just how they are, thank you very much. So does our brain for that matter. Mr Amygdala, who is at the helm of our primitive brain, doesn't like his boat being rocked either. Nevertheless, Mary's eight steps are most definitely highly recommended!

Colin and Mary are just two of the authors who talk about needing to be *willing* to forgive. It seems to crop up again and again, no matter which of the great teachers you happen to read or listen to. If you don't feel that you're ready and willing just yet, then just wait until you are. You will get there. It might help to think about what irks you as a bit like having to constantly carry around a brick everywhere you go. The longer you have to carry it, the heavier it will seem to get. How does it feel to think about never being able to put the sodding thing down? Many, many years ago, back when I was at university, the freshman lads from one the men's colleges there had to carry a house brick around with them as part of their initiation. From memory it was their constant companion for two weeks solid, and they literally had to carry it everywhere with them, not just around the college. They had to lug it with them around the whole campus as well – lectures, pubs, the lot. If they spoke to anyone, according to the rules of the initiation ritual, they had to introduce their brick to the other person, before they could continue the conversation. I think the idea was that the brick was thought of as more important than they were. After a fortnight of that, I don't think any of them would have been too sad to put the dang brick down and leave it far behind them.

Support And Challenge

The last process that I would like to introduce you to isn't strictly about forgiveness, but I found it to be very helpful nonetheless. A few years ago I got hold of a copy of Dr John Demartini's book *The Breakthrough Experience*, and worked my way through the "*Quantum Collapse*" process that he describes in the book. I also went to an event where he was speaking in Sydney a few years back. He's a great speaker with a very inspiring story! I've not done one of his Breakthrough Experience weekends, but I certainly recommend getting his book and working your way through the process to see if it helps.

One of the things that really resonated with me at his seminar is the idea that we are never challenged without being supported. Another version of that is that at the same time we are being put down, someone is lifting us up. In essence, the point he's making is that the good and the bad are happening simultaneously and are perfectly balanced. What's more it's this balance which makes up the divine order in our lives. So if you only ever see one side and not the other, you are living an illusion.

Dr Demartini is well known for the emphasis he places on values. He highlights the fact that each of us as individuals live by our own unique set of values, from the most important down to the least important. This hierarchy of values originates from what we feel we don't have. In other words, our voids determine our values. In our relationships we cloud the clarity of our own purpose when we compromise ourselves for someone else. I certainly can't argue with him on that one! When we are with someone who challenges our values, we become self-righteous and independent and expect them to live in *our* values. When we resent them (e.g. when they're putting the mortgage money on a box trifecta on race 3 at Rosehill) and close down to them, we're trying to get them to live outside *their* values. You can end up in a 'prey and predator' situation. If you're living your lower values you want to get pleasure and avoid pain. Unfortunately though, you can never avoid the pain. My notes from his talk say that addictive behaviour stems from a person's highest values being unfulfilled, and so they look for immediate gratification. Instant gratification was certainly what seemed to float my partner's boat, there's definitely no question of that in my mind.

So how does all this relate to forgiveness? Well, I think it's about coming to peace with the pain or the situation we're uncomfortable with. Dr Demartini's *"Quantum Collapse"* process is trademarked and copyrighted, so you really need to get the book or go to the seminar to get the details. It's another process that involves putting pen to paper, so I warn you it's not a purely intellectual exercise. It's quite cathartic to get your thoughts down on paper and see and hold then, as I found out when I was answering all those questions for my annulment application that I shared with you previously. The "collapse" part of the process refers to collapsing your false beliefs and illusions. Dr Demartini suggests doing it on someone who is 'pushing your buttons'. I'm assuming that it's conceivable that you could see your gambler as someone who is running your life, being in your way, or loading you up with burdens that you just don't need or want. There are a few steps to the process, but the guts of it is that you're aiming to come up with as many good traits of the person as you can bad traits. It's important that both lists are equal – you're balancing the bad with the good.

The next part of the process is to really see that you have the same positive and negative traits as the person you're doing the process on. Think about (and write down!) how it actually benefits you that this person has these negative traits. The idea is to keep going with your writing until you've dissolved any hatred or resentment towards the trait. Ask yourself how you having the same quality has served others. Ask yourself questions about the opposite quality of the person. For example, if you saw the person as stingy, then ask yourself who has perceived them as being generous.

There is a lot more to Dr Demartini's processes – make sure you read his book.

I can't help but share a final couple of quotes from John's Sydney talk to end this session off with: "Sit in inspiration, not desperation" and this little beauty: "Life is hell if you're ungrateful."

Resentment And Guilt

For an absolutely cracking take on the topics of resentment and guilt, see if you can get your hands on Bob Proctor's *"You were born rich"* programme. A quick google search should find it for you. The video footage of the seminar itself is quite something. It's a bit dated but the content is stellar and it's one of my favourites. In one part where Bob talks about resentment and guilt, it's extraordinary to see how they hold you back. He tells a story of how he used to suffer from migraines, and how he would take an astounding amount of painkillers just to be able to cope with them. One day when he was leaving a hotel to get to the airport, someone noticed how ill he looked. He told the man about his headache, and he responded by asking him, "Do you know what forgiveness means?" From the way he asked the question, Bob figured that he probably didn't, and so this man taught him that his head was aching because of the things he wasn't getting rid of. To get rid of headaches, forgive all thoughts in your mind that come to you. You can't live life by looking backwards, much like you can't drive a car forwards very well if your concentration is focused on what's in the rear view mirror. Bob's take home message is to stop looking back and worrying about something – let it go! In another five to ten years you'll likely find that that terrible thing that happened to you could well be the best thing, because advancement of all kinds is preceded by a crisis. So I want to urge you not to worry about the things that you can't change or alter. It's a bit like trying to change what you ate for breakfast this morning – with the best will in the world, that's just not going to happen.

Bob's take on resentment and guilt seems to be that they are essentially two sides of the same coin. Resentment is what you feel when you choose to build a negative idea around something that someone did to you. Any getting emotionally involved with that idea moves your body into a negative vibration. He calls resentment "a mental act of ignorance." When you play the same things over and over in your mind, you end up in the same vibration. You may well feel justified in holding onto your resentment, but it's a "dumb game". It's not our job to even up the score with the other person. The Universe will take care of that, so it's not our problem.

Guilt on the other hand, is just us looking back at something *we* did in the past, which *we* thought was wrong, reliving it all over again, and moving us into the same vibration that resentment does. Resentment is directed towards someone else, whereas guilt is directed towards yourself. You end up being the beneficiary of both, and neither is positive.

Another way to look at them would be to liken them to being in a prison. With resentment you can feel that the other person put you in there, but with guilt, you're in there because you put yourself in. Having locked yourself up, you've now got a good excuse to curl up in that small, restricting space and not risk expanding and making yourself bigger.

If you are into affirmations, one that Bob suggests is: "I willingly release the thoughts and things that have cluttered my mind."

Starting To Own The Self-Betrayal

Can you pinpoint the time when you started to compromise yourself in your relationship with your gambling partner? I think if we're honest, that's exactly what we did to ourselves even though we didn't think of it like that at the time.

"Our bitterness toward others indicates our lack of forgiveness toward ourselves."

—Maxwell Maltz

I can remember an incident fairly early on in the relationship that really took me aback at first, but then I seemed to do my best to suppress how I felt about it and think that just maybe, it was a one-off. And so the lying to *myself* began…

A short time after our marriage, my partner had to fill in a form for the Department of Immigration in order to get his permanent residency status approved. One thing they required were statements from two people who knew us both and could testify that the relationship was genuine. I remember my husband coming home from work one day and saying he'd got one of the guys there to sign his name to a story which was cooked up by them both over lunch. Apparently this man (who I'd never met) and I got on really well, and he was even a client of the business where I worked. There were also stories of some involvement I had with his pet dogs. Who knew? Well, not me, that's for sure! I wondered why he would even bother to go to the effort of inventing a story and then convincing a workmate to put his name to this work of fiction, when I had plenty of friends and relatives who actually knew us both. I think this is where I started to realise that this guy I married really *is* a bit dodgy and that realisation didn't sit so easily with me. Then I had to ask myself: how do I deal with this? The short answer is that I didn't.

I think this is probably where I started heading down the winding, shady path to compromise and betrayal of myself, all for the sake of not rocking the boat. Unfortunately, the more I had to try and hold the boat steady, the rougher the seas and the darker the looming storm clouds were becoming.

Every time we betray and compromise ourselves, we give away little bits of our power. Then when we later find ourselves painted into a corner and thinking "how on earth did I end up here?" The only person who we can really blame for the shoddy paint job, is ourself. As Oprah has said, if you don't pay attention to the whispers, the walls will fall down.

"You can't aim a duck to death."

–Gael Boardman

EIGHT

Shooting Ducks

WHILE THIS QUOTE from Gael Boardman may be very un-PC these days, he nevertheless hit the nail squarely on the head. If you want to change your current results, then it's no good just sitting there thinking about change and not taking any action. You're going to have to do some work to get whatever rewards you are after.

Sometime last century, I can remember my history teacher from high school telling us that history was really just the accumulated result of the decisions that people had made down through time; and I think he was quite right. By making a decision and taking action on it, people from the past set various chains of events into motion, which then interwove and became entangled with the outcomes from other people's decisions, creating the great big tangled ball of events that we call history- which with the benefit of hindsight we now take great delight in teasing apart to find where the starting point was. So, to make some history for ourselves, it seems that we will need to make some decisions and then take some action on them.

Given that you're reading this book, do you feel that it might be fair to say that you're not entirely happy and comfortable with the life of a 'Concerned Significant Other' of a compulsive gambler? Just like me, I'm sure you've got people close to you who aren't in the same pickle as you, and they seem pretty happy, don't they? When you picture your future in your mind, are you seeing it as rocky, uncertain and insecure? How does that make you feel? Would you prefer the feeling you'd get if you could see it as more secure and peaceful? Unless you grew up having a parent with a gambling problem, you likely as not had a lot of time on the planet where life didn't seem to be an endless cycle of worrying if there'll be any money to cover the rent, pay the electricity bill, buy the food etc. Mind you, when you were young, you probably weren't overly concerned about the future either, but can you feel the contrast of the two different life experiences?

Richard Branson said– don't lead sheep, herd cats. I think here the sheep are your feelings of overwhelm, your victim story. The cats are your motivation, your goals etc. -your thoughts and plans which you need to get in order.

As a wise man once said, you first have to know that you're in a prison before you can try and get out of one. To kick off then, how about we begin by figuring out what our starting position is, just like any self-respecting navigation app would do. If you are familiar with any of Bob Proctor's work, you may have heard him tell the story of a widow who took over her deceased husband's company, even though she hadn't had any experience or involvement with it previously. Despite their initial reservations, the company went on to do quite well under her leadership. Her secret formula for success was to ask the board members three simple questions every few months, and then let them get on with running the business once they had the answers. Her three questions to them were:

What are you doing?
What works?
What doesn't?

They sound pretty simple don't they? Simple, but effective.

Be fair, be kind, be true to yourself.

So if we can sort out where we're starting from, we then need to know the destination that we're aiming for. I don't think it necessarily has to be your end point. You may have a few places you want to visit along the way, just to break the journey up a bit and let you get some perspective on how far you've travelled and what the terrain up ahead may look like. I don't think you need to know *how* you're going to get to your planned destination either. You can feel your way and take notice of the pointers you'll be given along the way, the little nudges to go this way or that. For example, if you're driving home at night in the dark your headlights don't shine on your garage door when you start to drive off. They'll light up one bit of the road, and then another, and another. As you move forward the next road you need to drive along is lit up in front of you. The lights will show you where the potholes are, and where the crossroads are. They'll show you the stretches of roadway where you can safely speed up, and the narrow, windy parts where you need to slow down. If you just keep going where the headlights show you, you'll end up safely back home.

Decisions, Decisions, Decisions

Do you remember those questions that were asked back when I was sharing the annulment questionnaire with you? This part on decisions is going to be a bit similar. For example, it's not going to be like the type of work conference where you can just nod off in the lectures. This is the type of conference where the speaker presents you with a case study and expects the audience to put in a bit of effort and do some thinking to find the answers for themselves. I must admit, I used to prefer the former - the latter, not so much. If you haven't already done so, you're going to have to ask yourself some difficult questions, and no-one else can answer them for you. Deep down you know the answers though, even if they do push you out of your comfort zone.

"Failure means standing between two decisions."

–Maxwell Maltz

Life is in essence a continuum of change, so if we end up not doing anything, then we're actually making a decision to resist change. The reality is that if you're not moving that's not going to stop things moving around you. Think of your own body. Our cells are renewing themselves all the time as old ones die off and new ones are made that take their place. In six months from now, a year from now, you are going to be a different person whether you like it or not. Why not be the one who decides what your future looks like? I want you to keep that thought in mind as you consider the following questions.

- How long have you been thinking about your partner's gambling and how it makes you feel? Is it just a short while, or is it a long term thing? Should you be engaged to your unease by now because you've been living with it for so long? I read somewhere a long time ago that women who leave their husbands have been thinking about it for about two years. I believe that the time men think about leaving their wives is much shorter than this. Women seem to mull over it more than men do.

- What is the risk of doing something (anything) to change your present circumstances? What is the risk of doing nothing? How does the thought of doing or not doing anything make you feel? Do your shoulders tense up and gradually get closer to your chin? Does your stomach feel like there's a bowling ball inside it, weighing you down? Do you feel scared or excited?

- What do you think your options actually are? I think this is another exercise where physically putting pen to paper will help you enormously. Once you've got them there in physical form, it's a bit easier to take them one at a time, give them a good shake and see what falls out. Do they still stand up to scrutiny, or are some of them not realistic options at this point in time?

- If you think you've come up with some good options, why do you think you've not acted on these yet? What do you think it is that's stopping you from taking action on them?

Think about your dim, distant future. How close is that cardboard box under the bridge getting? Can you feel it getting soggy and leaking when it rains? How does it feel sitting in that cold, wet, sodden mess? Remember, in this day and age the captain doesn't have to go down with the ship anymore.

If you've decided to do something, how about you giving yourself a deadline to get it done. According to the old proverb, time waits for no man. I used to tell myself if things were still this bad in a year I'll leave. I have absolutely no idea why I picked a year. With the benefit of hindsight it seems like too long to me now, and a bit 'over the horizon' as far as seeing it happen was concerned. I'd suggest that you set shorter timeframes than a year. I think that way you're more likely to see some results and be encouraged to keep going. How about three months? Each of the seasons is three months long and then the weather is different, so how about we go with three months?

What Mother Nature Giveth, Father Time Taketh Away

Why is it a good idea to take some action after making your decisions? Well, we are all going to shuffle off this mortal coil at some point and Father Time's clock is ticking. When I was still in primary school my father was killed in an accident when he was only 38 years old. He and my mum went away to a family event and he never came back. I'm now older than my own dad was when he died, which is a bit of a weird feeling. Some years later when I was at high school, the girl who sat next to me in chemistry was killed in a car accident one night. She was young, bursting with life, very popular at school, and had already crammed an impressive collection of achievements into her short, bright shining life. I'm sure that neither my dad nor my chemistry buddy would have woken up on the day that they died, and had the thought that this was the last day they would ever have breakfast with their family. Since this trip we're on called life only comes with a 'one-way' ticket (as far as we know), maybe we should ask ourselves every so often if we are happy with the road we are on, or do we perhaps want to have a look at what's down the next fork we come to? Are we spending our time here as wisely and productively as we could or should? Remember the 'Days of our life' theme - "Like the sands through the hourglass, so are the days of our lives." Too true.

Driving Your Own Bus

Once you've decided to grab the bull by the horns and put your foot down with a firm hand, it might be time to tell yourself "This is **MY** bus, and **I'M** driving it!" I've pinched this phrase from a speaker at a conference that I attended many years ago. It was what he would tell people once he'd laid out all their options for a particular course of action, and they'd made their decision as to which track they'd take. It made a lot of sense. If you want an expert to do their job properly you can't keep butting in and disrupting them, you've got to let them do their job.

Gaining back control of my life was a great feeling! It brings great peace of mind along with it. When you have 'control' and 'peace of mind' getting on well together, their good friend 'security' comes along and joins the party as well. The buzz when these things all get together in the same room is just such a nice feeling!

The Sheep On A Different Track

Having made the decision to do something differently from the way you've been doing it in the past, you may find it a little difficult to leave the discomfort of your old 'comfort zone'. You may not have loved being there, but you knew the routine and choreography of the dance moves. It's a bit like sheep who follow the same tracks around a paddock. They may have a huge area to wander around in, but they have preferred pathways that they follow to get from A to B to C. Maybe you could be a rebellious sheep driving its own bus along a brand new track of its own choosing in the great big paddock of life.

Procrastination is a bit like not wanting to venture off your own sheep track. If you stay on it, it feels comfortable. You know what it looks like and where it's taking you. Heading off in a different direction can be daunting and maybe a bit overwhelming. There may be long term gain up ahead, but there's short term pain right in the here and now. It depends which pain is worse really; the pain of changing direction now, or the pain of regret further down the track if you don't change.

Your ducks are probably never going to be all lined up, so just go for it. Take the first step. Things will work out and fall into place when you make a decision to move forward and take action. Remember Newton's First Law – you just have to get yourself started.

Taking Ages To Find The Keys To Your Bus?

You may be procrastinating because that feels like the more comfortable course of action at the present moment. I think one of the best explanations as to why we procrastinate is the one by James Clear. His take on it is that we tend to care too much about our present self, and not enough about our future self. If the costs of our choices aren't going to come to the surface until far into the future, then we're quite happy to enjoy the immediate benefits right now, thank you very much. He gives us the example of eating a donut as giving us an immediate payoff, because we get a nice sugar hit, but the cost of slacking off with your exercise workouts won't show up until you've been skipping them for months. If we look at your problems in the distant future though, our choices will usually change. In 365 days you'll be a different person anyway, but would you rather be chubby and chuffing down donuts or would you rather be healthy and toned? Seems an easy choice doesn't it? The problem is that when we have to make a choice right now we tend to overvalue the immediate benefit of our behaviour and discount what it's going to cost us in the long- term. It's a tug of war between Future You and Present You.

Be Like Cliff And Edmundson

The point I want to make here is that slow and steady wins the race. Do you remember Cliff Young winning the Sydney to Melbourne ultramarathon back in 1983? It's the Australian version of the classic 'hare and the tortoise' story. At 61 years of age, Cliff just shuffled along the road from Sydney to Melbourne each day, imagining that he was out chasing his sheep. At the end of the first day he was trailing the rest of the field by quite a long way, but while the other runners went off to bed and slept for the night, Cliff just kept on going. He took the lead on that first night, and just kept trotting along for five days straight, beating the second placegetter to the finish line in Melbourne by ten hours and taking nearly two days off the record for the run between the two state capitals. Once the media got wind of the potato farmer outrunning the professional runners, we got to see footage of him on telly each night, chugging along in what looked like track suit pants with little holes cut out all over them. While he didn't seem to fit the usual picture of a marathon runner, his unusual technique blew all his fellow competitors away. By taking small little incremental actions, steadily performed with a clear end in mind, while blocking out any distractions, Cliff got there streets ahead of anyone else and took first prize.

About 70 years earlier than this and a bit further South than Melbourne, the Norwegian explorer Roald Edmundsen and the British explorer Robert Scott were both heading to the South Pole, and we all know how that ended up. Edmundsen got there first and made it back safely, whereas Scott and his team had a much harder time of it (for various reasons) and all perished on the return journey, carrying with them the knowledge that Edmundsen had arrived at the Pole before they did. One of the reasons for Edmundsen's success was that he and his team made steady progress each day. He'd come up with a plan to move one degree of latitude for each four days of travel, so that his men could imagine themselves moving closer and closer to the Pole by a quarter of a degree each day. Scott's team didn't have a set goal for how far they would travel each day. He did have worse weather to contend with than Edmundsen, but he had a different approach to making forward progress. When conditions were favourable he and his men would travel for up to nine hours at a time, and when the weather was bad, they often wouldn't leave their tent. Both teams had the same end goal of reaching the South Pole, but the Norwegians had a steady, incremental goal to achieve each day to help them get there, whereas Scott's team didn't.

Kaizen – The Japanese Art Of Improvement

Kaizen is a Japanese term which means improvement. It is usually taken to mean someone making continual, ongoing improvement in all aspects of their life – personal, social, home and work. The practice of kaizen calls for commitment to continual effort. Think of flowing water which over time carves out deep and winding rivers, or that well-known proverb from the Tao de Ching: a journey of a thousand miles begins with a single step.

Shrines and temples in Japan are often built in mountainous areas, and the most sacred altar is usually at the top. Someone who wants to pray at the shrine may have to make their way through a forest, up steep steps and go through many tori gateways. The well-known and very frequently Instagrammed Fushini Inari shrine at Kyoto has between 10,000 and 30,000 torii gates, depending on which guide book you read. It seems that they are constantly multiplying though, because if you've got the money, you can pay to have another torii gate put up along the way and have your company name on it. The gates lead up a hill, with lots of smaller shrines along the way. The idea is that by the time you reach the altar at the top, your soul is purified. The journey up to the top to the shrine is almost as important as the prayer you make once you reach it. This is a very popular shrine, with busloads of tourists visiting it, but the old saying that there's not much traffic on the extra mile is quite true here. I admit that I didn't make it all the way to the top when I visited, but certainly the higher I got the fewer and fewer people there were up there with me. I spent a lot of time stopping to admire all the statues of Kitsune the fox wearing his red bib, which are dotted along the way up the hillside, as well as meeting some cats at the little shops on the route. Alas, I failed to commit to the continuous effort that was needed to make it to the top as I got distracted along the way, but I feel that the journey was still very worthwhile. Perhaps your kaizen effort could be tucking away five dollars a week in a 'shy place,' so that if you ever need some funds to get away in a hurry, or to help you out of a tight spot then you have an emergency stash that can put your hands on if the need arises.

If you have committed to whatever goal you decided to set for yourself, your daily kaizen habit could be to get into the practice of writing down a list of the six most important things that you need to get done the next day to reach that goal, start with your most important task at number one and then working your way down your list to number six. If you don't get through all six, just move them to the next day's list. This idea earned Ivy Lee a check for $25,000 from Charles Schwab back in 1918, after Schwab's executive team at Bethlehem Steel used it for three months. I'm sure $25,000 was worth a buck or two a hundred years ago, and one can only presume that if he was paid that amount of money for it, Lee's idea must have generated some pretty impressive results for Mr Schwab and his steel business. With that kind of recommendation behind it, it would seem like an exercise worth doing. What's more, it hasn't cost you anywhere near $25K!

Finding Motivation

If you find it a little hard to take steps in a new direction, or do something that you may feel is outside your comfort zone, then you may need a bit of a prod to get you moving. Here are a couple of suggestions for motivators that may help you. Do you remember earlier when we talked about uncertain rewards and avoiding loss as being motivators for gamblers? Well, it turns out these will work quite nicely for non-gamblers as well. It seems that we humans will put in more effort to get an uncertain reward, than we will to get a certain one. For example, Fishbach explains that we'll work harder for a 50% chance of getting either $150 or $50 than we will for a 100% chance of getting $150. Go figure! We've all seen those queues out of newsagents when there's a big Lotto or Powerball draw on. People will line up to hand over some of their hard earned money to take a chance on winning a truckload of cash (as the ads say). So, if you need an extra incentive to get a bit of a wriggle on with whatever your particular project is, try putting $150 in one envelope and $50 in a second one (or whatever variation of these amounts that you can afford), mix them up and then choose one at random as your reward for completing your task.

As far as making use of our ingrained aversion to losing goes, Fishbach also reports that people would walk 7000 steps more often when they would lose $1.40 than when they would gain $1.40. That's a pretty small amount of money to be an effective motivator, would you agree? That small change will barely buy you a postage stamp. Instead of facing the prospect of losing $1.40, the author suggests that if you don't reach the particular goal you've set for yourself, you make a commitment to donate money to a political party that you don't like. Not a bad idea. I reckon that one might work. What do you think?

Beliefs

This might sound like a bit of 'woo woo', but stay with me here. Our subconscious paradigms control our behaviours. To change the results we're getting, we need to change our beliefs around certain things (like what we're prepared to put up with from someone else). To change our beliefs and paradigms, we need to start telling ourselves a story that's different from the one we've been telling ourselves up to this point in time. We can't 'see' another person's beliefs, but from what that person says and how they behave, we can usually infer what their beliefs are. Our beliefs about ourselves are what drive our daily actions, which add up to our weekly actions, then monthly, then yearly – you get the drift. Unless we make a conscious change to the way things are now, that's likely to be the way they'll stay until doomsday. If you're happy with the status quo then you don't need to do anything, but I'm assuming here that you're a tad hacked off with the current status quo and would like to make a few changes in your favour. So thinking of our gambling partner then, how can we either change our old beliefs or come up with new beliefs around the gambling and the associated behaviour that goes with it? Learning from our own personal experience is one way. There's nothing quite like 'living the dream' to make you feel as though you're actually living in a nightmare. If you want to pick the situation apart logically, that would work too. If you take the emotion out of the situation and try to look at just the facts you might start spotting the inconsistencies in your partner's stories or behaviour. Another way to change your beliefs is to accept the advice of someone you trust who is an expert on the matter – a gambling counsellor for example. Remember, if "The story never changes", then there's probably a very good reason behind that.

Placebos And Nocebos

Placebo is Latin for 'I will please'. Recent interest in this fascinating field was probably kick started by Dr Harry Beecher, an American anaesthetist who worked in military field hospitals in World War II. On one occasion he had a patient who needed morphine before a surgery, and Dr Beecher didn't have any. Instead, the nurse just injected saline, telling the patient it was morphine and it settled him down straight away. He seemed to feel little pain during the operation, and he didn't develop the full blown shock which Dr Beecher was expecting either. When the morphine supplies ran low in the months that followed, he repeated the saline trick (unbeknownst to the injured soldiers) and it worked like a treat again. Unlike real drugs, which we know will definitely work, placebos only work if you believe that they will, and it turns out that there's a hierarchy among placebos (at least as far as medicinal effects are concerned). At the bottom of the ladder we have plain white tablets. White capsules work better than white tablets, and coloured capsules work even better than the white ones. The creme de la crème of the placebo world is the injection.

If the placebo is like the favourite aunty who makes awesome cakes and who everyone loves, then the nocebo is the creepy old uncle that puts everyone on edge. Nocebo means 'I shall harm'. Examples of the nocebo effect include gypsy curses and bone pointing. For these curses to be effective people have to know that the spell has been cast, and they have to believe that it will work. In the case of bone pointing, people can die within a few days of being pointed. In his book *Living magic*, Donald Rose explained that the pointing was the first part of the killing, but the bone had to be "loaded" before it was able to kill. The 'clever-man' would chant over the bone and point it at the direction of the intended victim. The belief was that a 'shadow' of the bone had entered the victim's body. For it to work, the victim had to know that he had been pointed, and so he knew that he would die. The people around him knew it too. When the clever-man burnt the pointing bone, it burnt the bone in the other man's heart. His relatives would start to mourn him and he knew he was going to die. So he did. That's a powerful belief!

The Story Of The Frosties

I'm going to tell a tale on myself now. It illustrates how we can come to believe something that isn't true, and that appearances can be deceptive if we trust the person telling us the story. This dark tale centres around an empty box of Frosties cereal. The kids had run out of their breakfast Frosties one day, so I'd bought a substitute cereal which happened to be on special at the time. Said substitute was very, very similar to the Frosties, and in fact they'd both been happily eating the same kind of cereal some months earlier. The youngest one saw the box and immediately said "I don't like these. I wanted Frosties." So I went back to the pantry and grabbed the empty Frosties packet that had been kept for some kind of craft project, swapped the bag of substitute cereal over into it, and hey presto! Frosties for breakfast again! The eldest kidlet ate them no problem at all. The youngest one was a slightly different kettle of fish though. A sample of Frosties were poured out and examined. They were declared to be 'old' because they'd been at the top of the packet. Some more were poured out and the verdict was that "These aren't coated like Frosties." "Well," I said "Maybe they've just changed the recipe a bit?" Success! The substitute cereal was happily eaten until the box was finished, and neither of them even noticed that the picture of the tiger on the front of the box had already been coloured in by one of them.

So why did they believe it? The box said they were Frosties, so they must be Frosties. Even when one of them was highly suspicious, all it took was a throw away comment about a possible but fictional change to the recipe and the story was bought, hook, line and sinker, no further questions asked. The doubting Thomas had initially trusted what their senses had told them, but it wasn't that hard to steer a change of opinion. The other one just went with the outward appearances and was able to be sold on the idea very easily. So if you think something is a bit 'off' you may well be right – trust your gut.

Affirmations

Diving deeper down into the cool swimming hole in the world of Woo, let's have a chat about affirmations and how they work. Affirmations are positive statements that we make to ourselves on a regular basis that can change our beliefs about a certain situation, and so help bring about the results that we're after. They can also work in a negative way though. I'm sure we all know people who go through life saying "This is crap, this job is crap, my boss is a muppet, my wife is going to leave me, my kids are always causing me trouble, I never have any money, the government are bastards, etc, etc." The moral of this story is that they're usually right. Whatever we are constantly telling ourselves is likely to become a self-fulfilling prophesy. So why not tell yourself a good story instead of a not so good story? What have you got to lose? If you've been with your gambler for as long as I was, the answer to a question like that is probably "not much."

Some guidelines around making your affirmations more effective are to make them positive and frame them in the present tense. There are bucket loads of ready-made affirmations out there on every topic under the sun. You can either use ones you find that you like and that you feel resonate with you, or you craft some of your own so that they sound more like something you can hear yourself saying and that don't sound odd to you.

So why do affirmations work for us? Well, remembering that our subconscious mind is what drives about 95% of our actions, then we need to get our conscious mind to do some work on its subconscious counterpart that might not be supporting us to get to our goal. As an example of how the interplay between the subconscious and the conscious mind work, I'll tell you a little story about my grandfather. I can remember hearing a story about a time when he was a young boy, and he and a couple of his mates had some fun on the weekend by going to the local park where a brass band would regularly play. The story is that the boys would stand in front of them sucking lemons. This would mean that those playing the wind instruments would start salivating and wouldn't be able to keep playing. My grandad and his mates would get a kick up the backside and be moved along, but by then the lemon sucking had had the desired effect on those who weren't even sucking lemons! Can you taste lemon now?

For a brilliant explanation of how the subconscious and conscious minds work, I'm drawing on the work of the great Bob Proctor. There are plenty of videos of him on YouTube, so you might like to check him out at some stage. The basic point he makes is that you really can't nail down your 'mind' to being any particular part of your brain. The thinking is that your mind is actually spread throughout your whole body. I bet if someone asked you to draw a picture of your mind, you'd be hard pressed to do it. Dr Thurman Fleet, an American chiropractor, realised that as humans we think in pictures, and so he developed his concept of the stick figure to show his patients how their mind worked, and to explain to them how their thoughts were creating their future.

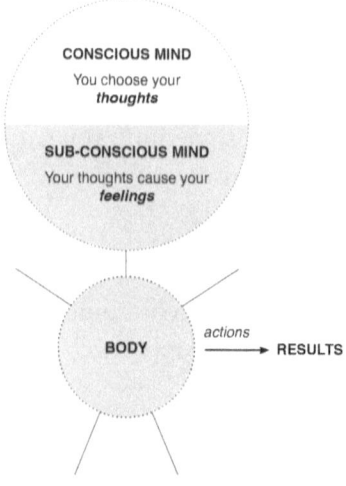

Your conscious mind is your thinking or reasoning mind. This is what is taking in information from your five senses about your environment. Your thinking mind can accept or reject what comes into it and it can originate thoughts. Your subconscious mind is your feeling mind. It has to accept whatever comes into it. It can't reject and it can't tell if what is coming into it is real or imagined. By listening to the same stuff over and over every day we form our paradigm, and our paradigm is what drives our actions. Changing our paradigm means that we need to constantly repeat the new information that we want out future to be shaped by so that we can push out the old information that is not getting us the result that we want. Out with the old and in with the new. Our self-image controls everything we do, and our self-image is part of our paradigm. If you want to change your life, you need to change your paradigm. You need to put your will in control of your mind, rather than running on autopilot. Bob has an awesome seminar on shifting your paradigm, and there are plenty of videos out there of that too. It can be painful to take an honest look at the results you've been getting up until now. Remember, to make a change, you've got to change your programming.

So you might be wondering if there is any actual evidence that our mind and our thoughts seep into all our cells and all our tissues, and don't just sit locked up in our brain? For me, thinking back to the nocebo effect of bone pointing is enough evidence. It seems to be that to be able to kill a person in a few days just with an idea that's transferred to them, means that there has to be some real physiological change in the body. That's the only way that a physically normal healthy person could be turned into a completely lifeless one.

A more contemporary example is provided by the cases where people who have received heart transplants find their personalities changed. There has been some very interesting work done by Pearsall and others on how some heart transplant patients have shown personality changes which parallel the history of their donors. A woman called Claire Sylvia wrote a book about hers. She was a very health-conscious dancer who received a heart and lung transplant in 1988. She found that after the surgery, some of her tastes, habits and attitudes changed. She went from having an aversion to beer and fried chicken to having uncontrollable cravings for Kentucky Fried Chicken nuggets, and she started drinking beer. Her clothing preference changed from bright reds and oranges to cool colours instead, and she started behaving with an aggressiveness and rashness that she'd never had beforehand. She was able to track down information about her donor and found out that he was a young man with the personality traits that she had acquired, and who'd had a hankering for beer and chicken nuggets. In fact some uneaten KFC nuggets were found in his jacket when he was killed.

Other examples described by Pearsall include a man who received the heart of a young classical violinist and then developed a love for classical music and whistled songs he'd not ever heard of before. Stories of child donors and recipients are fascinating too. One particular case is that of a 16 month old boy called Jerry who drowned in a bathtub, and Carter, the seven month old baby who received his heart. The recipient and donor families actually met, and Carter interacted with the donors parents the same way that Jerry had, and at six years old he used the same baby talk with them that Jerry had. On first seeing the donor's father, he went up to him, climbed on his lap and called him daddy. Jerry had had mild cerebral palsy on his left side, and after the transplant Carter developed some stiffness and shaking on the same side. Not everyone who has a heart transplant reports personality changes afterwards, but the fact that some do (around 16%), and that their new personality mirrors the personality of the donor is really quite fascinating. It opens the possibility of the idea that we carry cellular memory of ourselves in our tissues, which could explain why changing our subconscious paradigm is a whole body experience.

The queen of positive affirmations is Louise Hay, and her book and DVD *You can heal your Life* really set the pace in this area. In an interview with Oprah a number of years ago, she was asked what her top three affirmations were. Here they are:

—*All is well.*
—*Everything is working out for my highest good.*
—*Out of this experience only good will come and I am safe.*

Talking of Oprah, as you move forward out of the mucky mire of compulsive gambling and all its works and all its empty promises, take some advice from her about the people that she refers to as 'energy suckers'. I saw the following gem in an interview that Oprah was doing where she was talking about our energy and our personal responsibility to manage it. She talked about how we are responsible for the energy that we bring to other people and into the situations we are involved in, but also said that we also have to take responsibility for the energy which we allow to be brought into our own space. We can't keep moving forward if we are surrounded by energy that brings us down and sucks the life force out of us. So, just as we are responsible for the energy that we bring to others, we are responsible for the energy that we surround ourselves with. She says that "There are some energy suckers in your life just literally taking the life force out of you, and you will never be able to do and be who you are supposed to be in the world as long as you continue to buy into the energy suckers.

Be fair, be kind, be true to yourself.

So then, time to kick off your journey to personal transformation and freedom. The first thing to do is know where your starting point is, and know where you want to go. One way to get a handle on this is to ask yourself, what are you doing? What is working for you? What is not working for you?

Gratitude

Our last bit of woo woo is gratitude. Keeping a daily gratitude journal is something else that Oprah talks about, as do a lot of other very successful people. Being grateful for what we have is the foundation that seems to allow more good things to find us, which in turn gives us more to be grateful for. Some people suggest writing your gratitude list in the morning, while others suggest doing it at night as you reflect on your day. Whichever way you go about it, and however long your list is, I'd suggest adding one in there for what you are grateful for about yourself. While being grateful for the things you *have*, also be grateful for what you *are*.

The things that I've shared with you in this chapter may not necessarily be game changers, but I can assure you that the small incremental changes you make by adopting any or all of the things I share with you, will put you in a much better position to take back control of your life.

"When you combine ignorance with borrowed money, the consequences can get interesting.

—Warren Buffet

NINE

Money / Fun With Finance

WELL, here we are at last, staring at the elephant in the room. Money: the getting of it, the wasting of it and the rebuilding of it. With Australia having followed the UK and left the gold standard back in 1915 during World War I, these days money really is just a concept that everyone agrees to agree on. You can't take a $50 note to the bank anymore and ask for your $50 worth of gold. That polymer note in your hot little hand is just a tangible form of the idea of 'money'. And while everyone agrees to be on the same page about it, it's an idea that holds water and stops the masses from storming the banks demanding all their savings back. These days money is an electronic idea too. There are millions upon millions of dollars whizzing about in the ether, going into your bank account from your employer then going out again to pay your mortgage, buy your morning coffee, get the groceries after work, and pay the bills online at night while you do some shopping on your favourite online shopping site(s). Have you noticed that a lot of the time when you go to pay for something, the person behind the counter automatically pushes the eftpos machine over to you saying "When you're ready." If you hand them cash they look a bit surprised. While this electronic money transfer malarkey is very convenient, personally I still like the look and feel of cash. I think it makes your purchases seem more real when you have to open your wallet and take out the physical cash and hand it over into someone else's keeping, than if you just wave your mobile phone over a wifi operated pickpocket. Think of money like energy. It's easier to keep track of how you're using your energy if you can see it in front of you and you can feel it in your hand.

Compulsive Gamblers And Money

Here again, we all know how this story is going to end, but just to really cheer you up, let's have a look at some fun facts about gamblers and money. Henry Lesieur who is the author of *The Chase* tells us that it's not uncommon for problem gamblers to have loans from six or more different sources at any one time. In a survey of 400 members of Gamblers Anonymous in Germany, 55% reported that they had obtained money by illegal means. And compared with those who hadn't sourced money from dodgy dealings, the ones who *had*, reported that they gambled significantly more often and for longer with higher stakes and larger losses. Most of these illegal acts fell into the bucket of 'non-violent property offences' such as theft, embezzlement, fraud, forgery to documents and tax evasion. Meanwhile a minority of the respondents did admit to robbery or blackmail to get money.

A study of Canadian Gamblers Anonymous members covered by Ladouceur and colleagues found the following (and bear in mind that the gamblers may not have been 100% honest about the extent of their actions):

84% admitted that they had had to borrow money during the past year to gamble

62% had borrowed money from family and friends

20% had borrowed money from loan sharks

More than one third had stolen money from their employers to gamble with (that's a LOT of people with their hand in the till!), and two thirds admitted to illegal acts to finance gambling, so it's a bit higher in Canada when compared with their German counterparts.

Logically then, if you tell yourself that your gambling partner is absolutely not the type to pull something dodgy that could see them end up in front of a judge, then it's fair to say that you'd be right about a third of the time. How do you feel about those odds? If you were going into hospital for an elective surgical procedure and the doctors offered you a one in three chance of surviving, would that not give you second thoughts about whether you really needed to put your future on the line for something that wasn't strictly necessary?

If you're still with your gambling partner, I want you to think about how that makes you feel and act where money is concerned. I'll wager that you are hiding money away so that you can pay the bills and keep the lights on. Another uncomfortable question I have for you is whether you can go to the supermarket to do the grocery shopping and know that there'll be enough money to pay for it when you get to the checkout? I vividly remember being behind a well dressed, well spoken lady at our local supermarket when her eftpos card was rejected at the checkout. She was extremely embarrassed by it all and said that her husband must have taken some money out of their joint account without telling her. She ended up paying for her groceries with a credit card, and hurriedly left. Her shock and discomfort really struck me, and while I felt very sorry for her, I can recall feeling not so long ago that it could have been me rocking up to pay for a trolley full of food and finding out there was no money in the account to pay for it. It could easily have been me trying to sink through the floor with embarrassment. If you have ever been in a similar situation to that lady, you'll know *exactly* how she must have felt.

From what I've heard and read, gamblers allegedly do have some remorse and concern somewhere deep down about the enormous amounts of money they have wasted. From my own experience I'd say that I'll go to my grave being absolutely positive that this was not the case with my partner. He didn't give one iota of a stuff about the money. Talking of wastage brings me to another tip for you which I found out when I'd separated from my partner and I was arranging a binding financial agreement to cut the financial ties. The law in Australia where I am based is that you are entitled to an extra 10% on top of the split of any assets if you are married to a compulsive gambler or an alcoholic. This is related to what they call 'wastage' of the assets of the marriage and in reality it probably gets you an extra 10% of sod all.

Have you ever wondered whether your gambling partner is using money as a way to control you? If you have kids and you've separated (or are thinking about it), be aware that the payment of Child Support is something that can cause you a number of headaches if you have a private arrangement in place and the Child Support Agency (CSA) doesn't collect money on your behalf. There was a time when my partner wasn't paying any, because we'd had a new assessment from the CSA and he decided that he'd already paid me all he had to, so in his mind he was entitled to decide not to pay any more until about three months had elapsed, to cover the apparent over payment he'd already made. I'd had to go into Centrelink for something or other during this stretch of time, and they'd asked me about his payment of child support. When I told them that he wasn't paying any just yet I was told in no uncertain terms that it wasn't the government's job to support my children (which was absolutely fair enough) and that if I wasn't actively pursuing him for child support they would dock my payments. I was a bit taken aback by that. I wasn't really sure how one 'actively pursues' a compulsive gambler for money – I think the banks and loan sharks already have that market cornered.

I share this part of my story with you here to give you a heads up about the fact that the child support world is a bit murky, to say the very least. The easiest way around it is to have the Child Support Agency collect the money from the other parent on your behalf. You don't even have to be involved at all, so there's no having to ask for the payment or needing to remind them when they're late. This was one of the best decisions I made, and has saved me an enormous amount of hassle. Fifty bucks a week is just nowhere near worth the amount of aggravation it causes. On one of the occasions when we were swapping the kids over and he hadn't paid his child support I had a grand total of $3.10 in my pocket and $2.60 in the bank. That motivated me enough to ask for the $50 he owed, and I can remember him opening his wallet and it being stuffed full of $50 and $20 notes, with the fifties outnumbering the twenties by about three to one. He just took out a single $50 note and handed it to me. I would like to say here, that I'm absolutely not taking a swipe at Centrelink or the CSA. My interactions with both these agencies have by far and away been very positive and supportive, which is a great outcome, considering the range of people and problems they must have to deal with day in and day out. Don't be under any illusion though that the single parent pension is designed to keep you comfortable – it's not. In fact I think it's designed to keep you just enough above the despair line so that you're mentally fit to get out into the workplace to earn money so that the government can tax you to get money to pay the other people on the single parent pension. On a cautionary note, just be aware that if you do need the pension to help you along until you can get back on your feet, the government will ask many probing questions and will know more about you than your own mother by the time they are finished with you.

Talking of Child Support brings me to kids. My kids are truly the light of my life, but they don't half cause some anxious moments when they want to! At around the same time as our eldest started school, his father and I were going through the process of formalising the child care arrangements for them. In the agreements we were nutting out I'd asked to have a clause included which stated that the children were not be exposed to gambling. This was based on advice from the gambling counsellor I had seen. The school tuck shop was open one or two days a week, and I would sometimes give him some money to spend at recess or lunch. One day I'd given him the princely sum of fifty cents, and when he got home off the bus I'd asked him what he'd bought with it. The answer was "Nothing", because he'd lost it in a game of heads or tails with one of the bigger kids. Almost my first reaction was to say "For the love of God, please don't tell your father you've been playing two-up at school!" Not after I'd specifically asked for them not to be exposed to gambling when they were with him!

Sexually Transmitted Debt

This is a well- known disease, and trust me, you don't want to get stuck with this nasty little piece of work. Just like puppies and herpes, you should be prepared for them to be with you for life, not just for Christmas. Some months after my ex had left, but before we had sold the family home, I went along to a mobile phone company to get a new mobile phone plan and some mobile broadband. The cost of the combined plan was only $29 a month, and even though I was working part time and was on a single parent pension, I failed the credit reference check. This is where the joint account thing and having your name on a mortgage with them can come back and bite you. I can assure you that it's pretty deflating to fail a credit check for a measly $29 a month, so watch out for all the places where you may have your name on the same contract as your partner, and get it off as soon as you can. Better still, don't combine finances in the first place, although things like that are always easier to say in hindsight.

Even after our old joint account was closed and the house was sold and the mortgage taken care of, I found out that that the legacy of my partner's demolition of our credit rating stayed on our record with the bank. I had an account with the same bank, and had to go and see them some years later after some other jiggery pokery that my partner had been up to, and when they pulled up my account details, there were all the old closed accounts still sitting there. Even when they're done and dusted, they don't retire gracefully, they're still there giving you the two fingered salute.

If only I'd recognised it at the time, Postie was delivering the evidence of a stack of credit card debt to me right at my home. I was getting offers for new credit cards in the mail from a variety of banks over a fairly lengthy period of time. They were banks that I had either never dealt with, or who I hadn't banked with for about 10 years or so. I used to wonder how on earth are they getting my address? Do they just rifle through the phone book and randomly mail out credit card applications? Maybe they did, but in my case, as I later found out, they were all banks that my partner had a credit card account with. Hindsight always gives you 20:20 vision, and no doubt the banks got my name and address from his credit card applications. After all, if you're considering shelling out about $10,000 credit to someone you've never heard of it would be nice to know if there's someone else at home who's earning a wage and could possibly service the debt. Sad to say, it was quite a long time after I'd received all these unsolicited credit cards offers that the penny finally dropped. Sharp as a pound of wet leather, that was me! Oddly enough, I never received any more of these credit card offers through the post once we'd had to sell the house and I no longer lived at the same address as a compulsive gambler. These days the banks aren't allowed to send unsolicited credit card offers, but it's probably worth keeping in mind that if your partner is running a few credit cards so that he can rob Peter to pay Paul, then the institutions that have issued them may well have your name and address on file too.

Get Thee To A Financial Counsellor (Not A Nunnery)

Great financial counsellors are out there, and they are very helpful! When I was still with my gambling partner I went and saw a couple of these. Women's health centres and support services can put you in touch with them if you're not sure who you can trust. Various other groups like church-run charities are also likely to have them. The two that I saw were free of charge, so with any luck you won't have to stress about how you will be able to afford them. The help they offer is invaluable, but of course it only works if you actually listen to it and act on it. A word of advice though. It was many years ago that I saw these people, and definitely before there were children on the scene. They both seemed quite visibly relieved to hear that there were no children involved in the situation I brought to the table, so it may be that the advice or help that some get is slightly different if there are children to consider. I went wrong in a couple of places when I went to see them. Firstly, I think I secretly hoped that they'd suggest that I left the relationship, and then that would give me permission to get out. Neither of them did that, and looking back I don't really think it was ever their job to do that. The other mistake I made was not following this brilliant piece of advice that one of them gave me:

NEVER have a joint account with a gambler.

Hindsight always gives you 20:20 vision though, so my very heartfelt advice from one who's been there, done that and bought the t-shirt, is: NEVER have a joint account with a gambler. I know that seems quite simple when you see it in print and hear it in person, but when it came to putting it into practice it felt like an act of disloyalty and I couldn't go through with it. Being as averse to conflict as I am, I also was very reluctant to have to approach him with the idea that I wanted to close our joint bank account. The home loan was in both our names, and to be honest, I'm not really sure how you'd ever get out of that arrangement without selling the house, which for us later became a necessity anyway.

I can truly say with the experience of having 'lived the dream', that you ignore this advice at your peril! If you do choose to ignore it, you too may find out the hard way what the words "joint and several" mean on a contract. The great thing about gamblers is that they don't seem to give a crap about the financial abyss they fall into. What's more, they don't appear to be at all bothered about who they pull in with them either.

NEVER have a joint account with a gambler. As Warren Buffet says: It is impossible to unsign a contract, so do all your thinking before you sign.

This same financial counsellor who told me to never have a joint account with a gambler also told me that if your partner is racking up credit card debt here, there and everywhere, you can write to the relevant banks and let them know that your partner is a gambling addict and ask them not to offer more credit. Apparently once they've been advised of the situation, they're supposed to play ball. I'm not sure if this works or not, as I never followed through with it. Again, if I knew then what I know now I would definitely follow through, but back then, for some bizarre reason I was worried that it would be an invasion of his privacy. Mind you, having my own credit rating take a ride round the S-bend as a result of sexually transmitted debt was certainly an invasion of MY privacy! Still, I guess we all do the best we can, with the knowledge we have at the time. It's probably worth noting here that if the credit card companies can put a freeze on the accumulation of interest for gambling addicts, then it's fair to assume that it would be worth asking for similar treatment yourself, if you're in a position where you think you need that kind of help.

This wasn't the first financial counsellor that I saw. The first one was the one who gave me the *Serenity Prayer* handout, among others. It's funny how things happen sometimes. The Universe really does work in mysterious ways. My husband was out somewhere when I had the appointment to see this lady. As fate/luck would have it, I was just about to back out of the carport when he came home and drove up behind me. I had to ask him to back out, so that I could go. When he asked me where I was going, I stupidly told him. It was confronting and hard to tell him how worried I was about his gambling, and that I'd made an appointment to see someone about it. He wasn't at all impressed, and at this point he said to me what I thought at the time was the worst possible thing he could have said (I was wrong about this – he later said much worse!). He told me that I was the one with the problem, since I was the one that was worried about it. Wow! I wasn't expecting that at all, and it really rather floored me. Along with all the other warning bells that had gone off beforehand, this was like an evacuation siren going Woop! Woop! Woop! But did I listen…No. I dang well didn't.

So off I went to see financial counsellor number one. I don't remember much about this visit. She was a nice enough lady. I remember feeling that I didn't really hear what I was expecting to hear though, whatever that was, but she did give me some very helpful handouts, including the *Serenity Prayer*. Probably because I was so churned up, my strongest memory about this visit was that it turns out eucalyptus infused tissues are a *really* bad idea for a counsellor to have in their room. When you're crying and try to wipe your tears away with one of these little beauties, they make your eyes sting like a bastard! Take home message to counsellors everywhere – please don't put eucalyptus infused tissues in your consulting rooms!

Other resources for you to consider for financial advice include Centrelink. If you are on a pension, they run free information sessions on managing money and looking after your superannuation. A lot of superannuation companies offer these kind of sessions as well. Your local library will have books and magazines that you can read for nothing. Another free source of books and resources is university libraries. Although you won't be able to borrow anything unless you're a student or staff member, they tend to have a huge selection for you to choose from, as well as a nice comfortable environment to chillax in. These days the rules about eating and drinking in the library seem to be quite chillaxed as well, so you can hole yourself up and spend a decent amount of time in there if you ever feel the need.

If you want to learn about stocks and shares, the Australian Stock Exchange website has fee online courses that you can do to learn about them, and you can make up a dummy share portfolio to play with and see how you go. There are also small groups of likeminded people out there who form little share clubs. They all kick in some money and research the market and do some investing together as a group. I can't recall where I head this, but apparently women's share investing groups tend to perform better than ones that are run by men. I can't remember what the reasoning behind this is, but whatever it is, it sounds pretty positive if you're a woman and you're looking to join one.

This Be The Verse

Another way to think about money is to consider what your philosophy about money is. What are your feelings around it? Do you remember that stick figure diagram that we talked about in the last chapter? Up until the age of about seven, your little growing subconscious mind is wide open and just soaking up everything that happens around it like an obedient little sponge. It's not until we get to about seven that our conscious mind starts to come into its own and begins to think for itself. So thinking about how your parents handled money when you were a young child growing up is a worthwhile exercise to do. What were the money conversations like in your home when you were little and very impressionable? Was it that money is plentiful or scarce? Did discussions about it turn into arguments? Did they have little sayings about it that you heard over and over again that then formed your money paradigm? Little sayings such as 'Money doesn't grow on trees', or 'You have to work hard for money'. If you keep hearing these kinds of things over and over again then chances are that you will start to believe it. It's not your parents' fault if you've wound up with a scarcity mindset though. They were only doing the best they could with what they had at the time, and they were a product of their parent's thinking too. If you think about it, the money philosophy you inherited as a child could well have been the product of people who were dead and buried long before you ever came into the picture. Two parents made by four grandparents, made by eight great grandparents, etc, etc . You can see how that ends up being a lot of other people's ideas and beliefs around money that get filtered down to you in your impressionable young years.

A wise woman I know once described a wise man that I know as being 'tighter than a fish's bottom at 40 fathoms' (except she used a slightly different word than 'bottom'). I think I have also been blessed with a similarly watertight orifice. Meanwhile I acknowledge that holding on to money is not the same thing as growing it. Money is energy and you have to keep it circulating. Thornton Wilder and then Richard Branson both said things along the lines that money was like manure, in that piling it up in a heap will result in stinky smells, but if you spread it around it will help things grow.

Living with a gambler prompted me to pay more attention to just keeping my head above water rather than to cobbling together a life raft from the flotsam while the storm was still raging around me. I made decisions which in hindsight I would certainly question these days, but at the time they seemed necessary. At one point I cashed in all my long service leave while I was on maternity leave so that I'd have enough money to cover the bills. I guess it turned out to be a handy strategy at the time, considering what happened the week before baby number two was due on the scene.

Just in case the whole topic of money, or your perceived lack of it, is getting you a bit down in the dumps, I thoroughly recommend reading some of Stuart Wilde's books on the topic. Or better still, have a look at some videos of him on the net. Stuart has gone to join the choir invisible but I get the impression that he must have been a hoot when he was still here on this mortal coil. His description of the music in New Age shops will stay with me forever, and I don't think I can go into one without having a mental image of dogs. Stuart wrote a lot of books, but a couple of them that focus on money are *The trick to money is having some* and *The little money bible*. He talks a lot about spirituality and money, but he does it in a very down to earth way. Like a lot of teachers he talks about acting 'as if' by joining in and getting your senses involved in the whole feeling of abundance thing. Even if you don't have much cash you can do little things to get into the feeling of having money. He suggests going to the best hotel in town and ordering a coffee so that you can just sit there, soaking up the atmosphere of wealth and abundance. Listen to people's conversations and notice how they dress and how they carry themselves. In these kinds of places you won't find too many of them looking down at heel and whinging about the price of eggs. More likely they'll be discussing their business, talking about their holidays and socialising with people who are just as successful as they are.

As we stroll gently through the library of kindly meant and eminently helpful advice from people who have been there and done that, let's now sit down on our comfiest chair with a copy of Suze Orman's book *The Courage to be Rich*. This is an absolute gem of a book and is chock full for not just great advice, but also some excellent questions that will get you thinking about your relationship with money.

Suze's essential law of money after a loss is to do nothing with your money (aside from keeping it safe) for a minimum of six months, but up to a year. This is because we tend not to make stellar decisions when we're in turmoil on the inside. She says that as with any relationship, there should be a healthy amount of mutual respect when it comes to our finances. If you want your money to look after you, then you have to look after your money. Suze has some great ideas about how to come to an agreement about your joint finances and spending. If you're not sure how you'll feel sharing your money with another person, having been financially battered beforehand she suggests that you both hand over an agreed amount of your hard earned money to the other party and then sit back and let them spend it absolutely however they wish. When the spending is done, this is where the fun starts! You need to have a good look at what they spent the money on and pay very close attention to how that makes you feel on the inside. Do you feel as though they wasted your money? Could they have done more with it? Or are you feeling comfortable with how they spent it? This little exercise will give you an idea of how close or distant your values around money are with your partners, and whether or not your new partner's way of managing or mismanaging money is likely to get right up your nose or not.

If everything seems to be tickety boo and you decide to take the new partnership to the next financial level, Suze also has advice about deciding how the bills and other joint expenses should be divvied up. This is especially important if you both earn a different amount of money. Suze's idea for wending your way through this minefield is actually very simple. You just contribute equal *percentages* of your income, not equal *amounts*. To make the maths easy, let's say Sam and Pam have monthly expenses (rent, electricity, food etc) which come to $5000. After working two days a week for the tax man, Sam gets to take home $6000 a month. His partner Pam earns less than he does, but after also being gouged by the tax man, she gets to take home $3500 a month. Now we add their take home incomes together: $6000 + $3,500 = $9,500 a month. The next step is to divide the total of their joint expenses ($5000) by the total of their joint take home income ($9,500). This equals 53%. What this means is that as Sam needs to contribute 53% of his take home pay, he will be contributing $3,158 per month, and Pam will be contributing 53% of her take home pay, which is $1,842. This way we end up with Sam and Pam's $5,000 monthly expenses being covered by way of both contributing the same percentage from their take home pay. I think that this works out nicely, would you agree?

And remember – *NEVER have a joint account with a gambler!*

"Number one always comes first."

—Thomas The Tank Engine

TEN

Finding Serenity

SO WE'VE MADE it to the last chapter, and as we start thinking about where to now, I want to share a piece of wisdom from Thomas the Tank Engine with you. Who would have thought he was a philosopher! If there's one thing I had hammered home again and again as a result of having a partner with an addiction, it's definitely this one! He was super sensational at putting his own wants and needs above anyone else's.

Some months after he left, we had to sell our home and the kids and I ended up in a small rental flat. I can remember our son playing with a talking Thomas the Tank Engine toy which his father's mum had sent him for Christmas. When you pushed his funnel, Thomas would chug along and chant encouraging slogans at you. He had quite a few in his repertoire, but the only one which really stuck in my mind was *"Number one always comes first"*. I remember thinking how ironic it was that his grandmother had (probably unknowingly) hit that particular nail right on the head! I was constantly being reminded of her son, even when he was long gone!

I think the "putting number one first" lesson is a great one for all of us, though perhaps best in moderation and not carried to extremes!

When I was at university our college principal would say 'Balance girls, balance,' only she meant it in the context of balancing study and partying. Either one carried to extreme wasn't good. If we have kids to look after in addition to putting our lives back together, then putting ourselves first at times is something we absolutely need to do. When I was a young kiddie growing up, I used to frequently hear things like 'You're not the only pebble on the beach.' It can be hard to buck the training, but sometimes we need to. You can't look after young children if you're dog-tired and frazzled. If you collapse in a heap, what then happens to your kids? Or yourself for that matter? Be gentle with yourself. Have compassion for yourself, and give the Thomas philosophy a go occasionally.

Be Fair, be kind, be true to yourself.

Lessons Learned

If I was to sum up the key lessons I learned through my journey to freedom, I'd have to say that the biggest ones were mostly about myself. Especially about what I was prepared to put up with, how much of my own power I was prepared to give away, and how far I could push my comfort zone to get myself to a better place. You've got to drive your own bus. It's not your job to fix someone's gambling problem, especially when they don't believe that they have a problem in the first place. As the late Stuart Wilde used to say, "What it is, is what it is." Everyone we meet is on their own journey through life, and came here with their own lessons to learn. It's more than likely they are different from yours, and in trying to help them, you are probably no help at all. I really used to have my head in the sand about my partner's gambling. If you feel that you may be doing the same thing, then the time to face facts is upon you.

I know that it's not necessarily going to be easy, but I also know that it will pay you back in spades if you learn to ask yourself the difficult questions that need asking. A counsellor that I saw after my husband left was absolutely brilliant not only at listening to me, but also at asking me questions as simple as "Why do you think this?" or "Why do you say that?" She helped me enormously, and I think a large part of that was down to the questions that she asked which forced me to look inward and search for the answers within myself. I knew she was good, because I'd sometimes talk to my ex about our sessions and things we'd talked about and he would get cranky and say to me "Your counsellor is shit!" That had the effect of making me think "Wow, she really must be good then!" which I doubt very much was the effect that he was aiming for when he said what he did. I suspect that he could see that he was losing control, and that didn't seem to be going down well. Remember that the only person on the planet that you can change is you, and no-one else. It's not your partner's job to look after you and make you happy – that's your job. Remember Thomas the Tank Engine. Number one always comes first.

What I want you to know is that (as preposterous a statement as this may sound right now), you can lose everything and still be OK – it's not scary anymore. You will be able to feel comfortable that you really can cope with whatever may be around the corner for you. I may have lost my husband and my home, almost had to ditch my career, not to mention the absolute crapload of money that went round the s-bend, but none of all that was fatal (either on its own or taken all together). Most self-made millionaires/billionaires have been made bankrupt along the way, some more than once. We learn from our mistakes. The person who never made a mistake never learned anything, and don't worry, you'll learn plenty. Learn to take risks. Gamblers seem to have no problem with this whatsoever. It may feel safe not to take risks, but you're also not going to achieve much either. You need to prepare yourself for your future. Mother Nature gives you a body and a brain to work with, but Father Time slowly steals these away from you. The time to move forward is now. Be grateful for the present moment. The children you ate breakfast with before school today will be slightly different children tomorrow morning, as they have their own learning experiences each day when they go away from you. Enjoy the moment.

At times it may feel as though you're making slow progress or maybe even no progress, but you are. It may not be obvious at the time, but when you look back you'll be really amazed at how far you've actually come. You may feel like you're going up and down hills and around in circles, but in actual fact you end up a long way from where you first started and you'll find that you've changed along the way. You'll be a different person, and you can never go back to being the person that you were back then. What's more you wouldn't want to. You'll find that you are much bigger than the space that you used to occupy and it would be a very uncomfortable squeeze yourself enough to go back there.

One of the things that will help you to navigate rough waters is to make sure that you have a soft place to land. Oprah talks about this, and about being a soft place for others to land. This is so very, very important. I'm truly blessed with a wonderfully supportive family, great friends, and the most awesome Mother's Group on the planet. I really want to urge you to do your best to develop a support group around you. When you've been in the dark, you'll really appreciate the light. In a blackout at night, a single match makes a huge difference. What you will find is that these people are absolutely invaluable to you when you need help and support the most. I want to give a big shout out to Mother's Groups everywhere. As I mentioned above, I am truly blessed to be a part of the most awesome Mother's group in existence. These ladies are an absolute godsend!

Another thing that I recommend is when you feel ready for it, get counselling, (both the regular and the financial kind). You'll know when you're ready for it. You have to be in the space where you're open to it before you'll willingly take it up. Back when I was at university, if you stood in one place looking at a noticeboard for any length of time, you would be pounced on by an eager Christian wanting you to come to their bible study group. They seemed to be like the tardis - they could literally materialise out of nowhere. And because I was typically engrossed in whatever I happened to be reading, my response was usually similar to what happens when you think a spider has landed on you! If Bible study groups weren't what floated your boat, these people were just plain annoying. It's the same when you are offering help to other people (including your gambler). If they aren't interested in your 'help', you're simply going to annoy them and they'll just get their back up and dig their heels in.

Even if you do have wonderful support people around you, I think it's worth having a 'worry tree' at home. This is a tree/bush/shrub near the spot where you get out of the car and go inside the house. When you come home, symbolically hang your problems on your worry tree and leave them there. Don't take them inside. I don't know who came up with the idea of the 'worry tree', but it's a great one. Also you can talk to your houseplants if you need to. Apparently, Prince Charles talks to plants and trees. I understand that people used to make fun of it when he was younger, but he's doing pretty well for himself it would seem. You'll also reap benefits from getting out into nature and the fresh air and getting some exercise as much as you can. If you have a pet at home, feel free to talk to them as well. They're great listeners and you know they're not going to run down to the pub and tell their mates what you've said.

Don't be like the cat that you read about earlier— the food bowl isn't empty, you've just convinced yourself that it is. The reality is that opportunities are everywhere, but you can't see what's out there when you're stuck in a bucket of stress, worried about what's going on right here, right now. The higher up the mountain you go, the better the view and the clearer the air is. Don't stay stuck in the boggy stinky swamp. Remember, you're not a tree. You can move and you can make choices.

Another thing I'd suggest that you consider is whether you are carrying your garbage around with you? In my council area, they collect your garbage once a week. As long as you (or the kids) remember to put the bins out, the garbage is gone the next day! We don't hang onto it and make an art installation out it, and then go out and polish it whenever we think of it.

You'll remember the chapter you read earlier on forgiveness. So if you haven't done it already, give yourself some space to forgive the gambler, forgive yourself and move on. Remember, it's only a wasted crappy experience if you don't learn anything from it. I don't know who said it first, but things don't happen to you, they happen for you, and everyone we meet is doing the best they can with the knowledge and inner resources what they have. You have to find a place inside of yourself to process the hurt. In some form or another it will always be a part of you, but don't let it destroy you. Don't go out into the world being angry. Rather, go out looking for opportunity and expecting good things to come to you, and they will.

Fine tune your 'crap-o-meter'. Learning to trust your gut and be honest with yourself is so important. If you can't be honest with the most important person in your life, then you're a bit stuffed really. Remember to watch what they do, rather than listen to what they say, and learn to say "Yeah? – No!" so the next time someone says "Step into my white van with no windows!" by now you're in a position to know exactly what they mean, and you won't fall for that old chestnut ever again.

Things I Used To Be Worried About That Turned Out Not To Be Worth Worrying About

I used to worry about what people would think of me if I left my husband. With any luck (and a bit of work on our mindset) we can get to a point in life where other people's opinion of us doesn't matter any more. I can attest to the fact that it's worth putting the work in to say that what others think of you is none of your business. Whatever you do, don't let pride or fear of humiliation get in your way or stop you.

Another thing I worried about was how I would cope on my own. As it turns out I actually coped pretty well. The opportunities that have come my way and the doors that have opened up would never have happened if the status quo had remained as it was.

Things I Don't Miss

I definitely don't miss freaking out when the phone rings, worrying that it's someone chasing him for money. I also don't miss getting text messages from the bank telling me that "account ending in xxx is overdrawn again, do something about it". These days I know exactly what is coming out of my bank account and when, and I'm not worried I'll have my card rejected at the checkout when I go to buy the weekly groceries

Last but not least, I don't miss covering up for him and hiding his gambling from my family, friends and work colleagues because I didn't want to look like a twonk for staying with him.

Things That Weren't Easy

No matter which way you look at this, being a single mum is a tough gig. I don't think anyone who has actually been one would ever say that it's easy. I can't remember where I read this, but somewhere in my past I came across the writings of a wise woman who said before you get married, ask yourself if you're prepared to live on your own. And before you have children ask yourself if you're prepared to raise them on your own. These are simple yet very profound questions that you should really take the time to think over. Sadly I haven't been able to track down who originally said this, as I'd very much like to give her the credit that she is due. She obviously knows just what hard work being a single mum is, and the degree to which it hurts right down to your soul when you worry about your kids. They never asked to be put in the situation they are in, but they are certainly embedded in it and have to deal with it. People can help in many ways, but at the end of the day, we can only move forward and grow through things like working through the grieving process ourselves. No-one else can do our exercises for us, just as no-one can diet for us. The reality is that crap happens to everyone - no-one is immune. All you can do is help your kids to make it through to the other side stronger for the experience, or at least with more resilience for their own journey through life.

Family Court wasn't easy either. In fact after the experience I'd say that I regard these as two of the scariest words in the English language. If at all possible, I recommend that you avoid the whole Family Court circus. It's a debacle. You're like the work experience lion tamer and they send you into a cage with the most hacked off of lions with nothing more than a fresh steak to defend yourself with. Believe me, it's a slow and tortuous death. The most ferocious lions are the ones that come from the Family Assessment Centres. If you see a lion with this name tag on, run like hell! I think the most pleasant thing a person from one of these centres said to me during her brutal verbal assault and battery was, *"Plenty of people don't have parents. Their parents are dead. How do you think they cope?"* I'm not the only person to have a shocking experience with the Family Assessment people. I was warned about how they operate, but I thought that it couldn't be as bad as it sounded. Wrong again! I think this lot must have learned their people skills and done their compassion training whilst serving in Hitler's Youth Movement. They will also misquote you and make stuff up for their Enid Blytonesque 'report' to the Court. I didn't believe this one either, but sadly it turned out to be quite true. Beware of them at all costs. Lions one, Christians nil is as good a score as it gets. If your expectations are lower than shark poop sitting at the bottom of the ocean, I can guarantee that you won't be disappointed.

So Where's The Serenity?

The good news is that (so far) I haven't ended up living in a cardboard box under a bridge! Hoorah! I can assure you that the Universe always has your back, and is always there supporting you.

After our family home was sold and the debts were paid off, I went looking for a little place for the kids and I could call home. I found a little old house in a quiet area that I was able to afford a deposit on. It wasn't flash, and needed some work, but it did the job. It had been in probate limbo for a couple of years, so I may have been in the right place at the right time when I found it. Not knowing when settlement would actually happen, the real estate agent who sold it to me told me that they would be closed between Christmas and New Year. I expected a lot of businesses would be, so I wasn't surprised. The conveyancer that I used also told me that she wasn't going to be working between Christmas and New Year. Fair enough, I thought, no problem. So take a guess as to when the stars all aligned and our new little home ended up settling…well, it was a date between Christmas and New Year. Settlement happened, the conveyancer attended, and the real estate agent handed me the keys to our new home a year to the day that my husband had walked out and left us.

I want to wish you well on your journey to freedom, and invite you to listen to the Universe carefully and see if you can hear Darryl Kerrigan saying "How's the serenity?" My parting words to you dear reader are, that you deserve to step up and claim your own sense of serenity.

Acknowledgements

Writing this book and sending it off for publication was harder for all those who contributed to its birth than we had ever imagined at the start of the journey. It feels as though we are sending our very dear and very precious only child off to kindergarten, knowing that we are gently pushing our little one out into the world in the hope that they will grow into a compassionate, patient and gentle global citizen who opens wide their arms to offer comfort, hope and most importantly understanding to all those who may need and welcome it.

A million "Thank You"s to Jane Turner for your unfailing faith and support at all steps in the production of this book. You have been an absolute rock. We are forever grateful.

References

American Psychiatric Association. (2013). *Diagnostic and Statistical Manual of Mental Disorders.* (5th Ed.).

American Psychological Association. (2015). *Dictionary of Psychology.*

Brown, M. Problem gambling a self help guide for families. The gambling Impact Society NSW.

Brown, R.I.F.(1993) Some contributions of the study of gambling to the study of other addictions, in Gambling behavior and Problem Gambling (eds W.R. Edington and J. Cornelius), University of Nevada Press, 341-372.

Bullock, S. and Potenza, M.N. (2012). Pathological gambling:neuropsychopharmacology and treatment. *Curr. Psychopharmacol.* Feb:1(1)

Dickerson M.G. (1979) F1 schedules and persistence of gambling in the UK betting office. *J. of Applied Behaviour Analysis* 12, 315-323.

Deutsch, A. *Change or Die*

Evans, D. (2003). *Placebo: the belief effect.*

Fishbach, A. (2018). How to keep working when you're just not feeling it. *Harvard Business Review* pp. 138-141

Ladouceur, R. Boisert, J-M, Sylvain, C. (1984) Social cost of pathological gambling. *J Gambling Studies.* 10:399-409

Lesieur, H. (1984). *The Chase: Career of the Compulsive Gambler.*

Lobsinger and Bechett. (1996). Odds on to break even: a practical approach to gambling awareness. Relationships Australia (Qld). Cited in: Petry N.M. Pathological gambling: Etiology, comorbidity and treatment. 2005.

Lorenz, V.C. and Yaffee, R.A. (1988). Pathological gambling: Psychosomatic, emotional and marital difficulties as reported by the spouse. *Journal of Gambling Behavior*, 4: 13-26

Office of Gaming and Racing, Victorian Department of Justice (in: Senate Committee – gambling reform report 2012)

Orford, J. (2001). *Excessive appetites. A psychological view of addictions.* (2nd ed.). Wiley.

Orman, S. *The Courage to be Rich.*

Padwa, H. and Cunningham, J. (2010). Addiction: A reference encyclopaedia

Pearsall, P. Schwartz G and Russek, L. (1999) Changes in heart transplant recipients that parallel the personalities of their donors. *Integrative Medicine.* 2:65-72

Rose,R. (1957) *Living Magic.* Chatto & Windus, London, 1957

Sylvia, C. (1997). *A change of heart.*

Vrij, A. (2008). Good liars. *Scientific American*, pp. 378-381

Wray, I. and Dickerson, M.G. (1981) Cessation of high frequency gambling and 'withdrawl' symptoms. *British journal of Addiction*, 76, 401-405.

Suggested Resources List

You can heal your life. Louise Hay. Both the book and the movie.

Weight loss for the mind. Stuart Wilde

You were born rich. Bob Proctor

Psycho-Cybernetics. Maxwell Maltz

The Secrets of a Bulletproof Spirit. Azim Khamisa and Jillian Quinn

The Magic of Thinking Big. David J. Schwartz

The Magic of Believing. Claude M. Bristol

The Power of Now. Eckhart Tolle

The Power of Intention. Dr Wayne Dyer

Who Moved my Cheese? Spencer Johnson

Mindset. Carol S. Dweck

The Biology of Belief. Bruce Lipton

Breaking the Habit of Being Yourself. Dr Joe Dispenza

www.ingramcontent.com/pod-product-compliance
Lightning Source LLC
Chambersburg PA
CBHW022017290426
44109CB00015B/1204